THE CHURCH THAT
CHANGES THE WORLD

A STUDY OF ACTS

KIE BOWMAN

Auxano
PRESS

ISBN: 978-0-9889854-9-0

Published by Auxano Press, Tigerville, South Carolina.
www.AuxanoPress.com

Contents

Dedication

This book is dedicated to our three children:

Amanda, Laura, and Joseph.

I love you all.

Acknowledgments

I want to thank some important people who have, in their own ways, contributed to the completion of this work. First, I am grateful to the congregation I have served for almost nineteen years. Hyde Park Baptist/The Quarries Church is one church in two locations, and together we have endeavored to live by the principles found in the book of Acts. They allow me the time I need to write, in addition to my other responsibilities as a pastor, and I am deeply indebted to these wonderful people. They are family to me.

I also want to thank the church staff who supported me through the writing of this manuscript. They seemed to understand when, at times, I had to leave meetings early, postpone a conversation, or ask one of them to fill in somewhere for me when I was nearing the deadlines that come with this kind of project. They are a great team to work beside.

A special thanks is owed to my executive assistant, Becky Shipp, who retyped chapters while looking for (and finding) grammatical mistakes, endured multiple revisions and corrections, listened as I obsessed about what I wanted to say, and constantly helped me carve out room in my schedule to make sure I reached the finish line, all the while freely commenting about the chapters she liked the most and why. I appreciate her professional assistance, and without her help I could not have finished on time.

The cover art was developed by Stephanie Cantrell, who showed remarkable alacrity in imagining a concept that helped to tell the story of the entire book at a glance. She is a gifted graphic artist and I appreciate the opportunity of working with her on the project.

I am also grateful for the team at Auxano Press for the opportunity to partner with them as we help people grow in their knowledge of the Word of God. My long friendship with Dr. Ken Hemphill has been extremely rewarding on multiple levels, and I am thankful for his encouragement through the years.

As always, I am grateful for my wife of thirty-five years who listens as I talk about what I write, long before I write it. She has heard nearly every thought I've ever had, and as the deadline for completion grew closer she seemed to grow in her sympathy for the urgency of writing. Fortunately, her patience increased as my time decreased. I am thankful to her more than I can say. She is an incredible person.

Introduction

The New Testament has twenty-seven books but only nine writers. Matthew, Mark, James, and Jude each wrote one book bearing their names. No one knows who wrote Hebrews. Peter penned two brief volumes; John added a long gospel, three small letters, and Revelation That leaves Paul and Luke who wrote the rest.

Of the twenty-seven books, Luke and Acts are the two longest. In fact, Luke's two volumes include more words than Paul's thirteen letters. The New Testament has a total of about 138,000 words. All thirteen of Paul's letters total less than 34,000 words while Luke's two books total about 38,000 words. Simply stated, Luke wrote more of the New Testament than any other author including Paul. Statistically speaking, Luke wrote 27.5 percent of the New Testament.[1]

The only reason to highlight this comparison is to expose a fact that seems hidden in plain sight. While Paul wrote more books and is rightly regarded as the most articulate proponent of the message of Jesus, Luke's massive contribution should attract more of our attention than it usually does as we consider the overarching message of the Gospel. After all, these two authors alone wrote nearly 60 percent of the New Testament.

---

[1] Felix Just, S.J., PhD, "Greek," New Testament Statistics, accessed February 15, 2016, http://catholic-resources.org/Bible/NT-Statistics-Greek.htm. (accessed February 15, 2016)

What does Luke's mammoth contribution to the New Testament add to our understanding of the Christian life? For one thing, we ought to study his writings more closely as we attempt to contextualize our faith in a culture that almost daily grows more indifferent and hostile to the Christian message. Luke understood the clash of ideology and culture. He lived and wrote at a time when the Jewish mind, the Roman world, and what was left of the substantial Greek influence were distinctly different and active worldviews. They were all simultaneously competing for the loyalties of the same people the early Christians were seeking to persuade. In many instances, the clash between those rival worldviews had deadly consequences for the Christians!

Therefore, Luke was no stranger to cultures in conflict. In light of this, if we want to navigate the choppy waters of cultural change more successfully today, we must better understand Luke's assessments and apply his conclusions concerning the phenomenon of the church's rapid growth in hostile territory. For this reason alone, if for no other, Acts has never been more valuable to the church than it is today.

In attempting to summarize Acts into a small volume (Acts itself is almost as long as this book about Acts) I have chosen to review twelve events that not only move the action of the narrative but, more importantly, demonstrate the seismic shifts of change brought about by the Gospel as it raced across the Roman Empire. Each of the chapters analyze the incremental, but enormous, steps the followers of Jesus took as they moved from a small, underestimated Jewish minority community to a worldwide movement in a single generation.

Luke intends for the reader to recognize these progressive steps, and he brilliantly documents, in compelling story form, the stunning advance of the Gospel as it marched from Jerusalem "to the end of the earth" (Acts 1:8). The early church's persistent obedience to the mission of Jesus produced dramatic change, not only in the world it influenced but also internally, as the church itself often experienced changes it did not immediately expect. The church's struggle to both obey the call of God, and at the same time adapt to its own growing understanding of God's worldwide agenda, is unapologetically played out in full view of the reader. We are privileged to witness those first believers grow numerically as well as in their comprehension of the mission itself. Only Luke provides this front row view of the history of the early church as it was being lived and as it matured.

For instance, Luke's record of the church's ever-developing understanding of itself and its purpose in the world begins in the first chapter, as the disciples immediately misunderstood the purpose of Jesus' resurrection. It continues on through incidents such as Peter's initial rejection of the message of the "unclean" food in the sheet let down from heaven (ch. 10), and it is brought into a brighter light when the Jerusalem Council convened to decide if Gentiles should become Jews first before they could become Christians (ch. 15). It is easy to forget the answers to the questions faced by the early church did not come neatly packaged in a thick volume of Systematic Theology. Instead, the early church constantly wrestled with what they were to do and how they were to do it. Yet, in spite of a few awkward moments of growing pain, God changed the world through the church.

Luke shows us that entire struggle, even while the gospel kept moving across cultural and internal barriers, forcing change wherever it went. The processes and progress of the early church should, therefore, constantly inform us as twenty centuries later we are forced to come to terms with challenges brought to bear upon our faith. During seasons of rapid cultural change, as the church finds itself in today, the book of Acts, which grew out of the same kinds of challenges, draws for us an increasingly relevant map for the way forward.

It is also obvious to the reader that Luke intentionally divides the book into essentially two complimentary biographies. By that I mean, in the earliest days when the church saw itself as a Jewish mission, Peter was the clear leader and the most visible main character. Mid-way through the book, when the church started to see its responsibilities to the Gentile world, Luke shifts the focus, subtly at first, almost exclusively to a Gentile mission. Paul is the main character then, and Peter fades from view.

Readers must remember that other ministries and missions were occurring at that time in history. The other apostles were actively doing their work, about whom Luke says very little or nothing. The absence of even a passing comment about the ministries of most of the other apostles is deliberate because Luke is almost exclusively concerned to show how Paul, introduced in the first third of the book, blazed the trail of the church into the Gentile world. Acts, therefore, is not a comprehensive history of the early church. It focuses primarily on the ministries of two men. Peter exercised a foundational mission to the Jewish people, and Paul led the larger mission to the Gentiles of the Roman Empire.

So, in light of the different possible ways to tell the story of Acts, this small volume seeks to demonstrate a simple premise: the early church changed the world in spite of the overtly resistant cultures where it flourished and grew. In the same way, the church today can shape and change the culture surrounding us, which appears, as it did in Luke's day, to regard our gospel as alien, unwelcome, and easily overpowered. The church in the first century was not overpowered, however, and Luke's boldly optimistic message is a reminder to a battered church today that in a world of competing ideas, a resurrected Savior is still a superior advantage.

In writing these chapters and retelling this story, I have attempted to shy away from heavy reliance upon the excellent commentaries on Acts. Instead, I have tried to inject as much *original* thinking into the work as is possible, based upon reflection and the clear reading of Luke's text itself. At the same time, I acknowledge the virtual impossibility of this approach, given the fact that I have been fascinated by Luke and have been studying and preaching from Luke and Acts for more than thirty-five years. As a result, the thoughts I have somehow convinced myself are my own are actually on loan from the much more able insights and scholarship of F. F. Bruce and his volume on Acts from The New International Commentary on the New Testament, I. Howard Marshall's

Acts in the Tyndale New Testament Commentaries series; John R. W. Stott from *The Message of Acts* in the Bible Speaks Today series; and John B. Polhill's commentary on Acts from The New American Commentary series, and many others. Where necessary, therefore, I have cited appropriate references.

When discussing Greek word meanings, translations, and syntactical issues, I have not attempted to cite every reference because, in most cases, the information is generally accepted and can be gathered from any number of sources. I do, however, acknowledge my regular use of the online language resource found at Blueletterbible.org. In addition, where needed, I have cited specific references related to linguistic issues if the insight is particular to a specific author, although this is rare.

The book of Acts was written two thousand years ago to demonstrate how the power of the gospel of Jesus Christ changed the entire world. More than at any other time in my memory, the church today needs to recover the passion for prayer, dependence upon the Holy Spirit, and the unreserved zeal of the early pioneers of the church. God used the original church to change the world, and He can still use the church to change the world. Do you believe that? After you read this book, I hope you will.

Chapter 1
The Power That Changes Everything

Acts 1:4-9

Mike was loud, negative, and argumentative. We attended the same college and on a small, Christian campus he was hard to avoid! One day he walked into my dorm room and started casually talking. It was obvious something was different. He was calm, not angry, and talking in a quieter tone. As I listened, he had a story to tell. The previous Sunday in church, he had asked God to fill him with the Holy Spirit (Eph. 5:18). Observing him for the rest of the semester proved that it was more than a passing enthusiasm. Mike had been changed by the power of the Holy Spirit.

Jesus spent about three years with a group of sometimes rough and rowdy men who could be spiritually awkward and, at times, even dense. In some ways, the men around Jesus were the least likely team to carry the message of salvation into the Roman Empire. Jesus knew that. They had spent every hour with Jesus since He had been baptized in the Jordan River and stayed with Him until His arrest in the Garden of Gethsemane. Days later they were the eyewitnesses to His resurrection (Acts 1:21-22) but, surprisingly, they were unprepared to tell His story and unqualified to receive the baton of leadership Jesus wanted to hand them. They needed more. They needed power.

Confusion About The Power (1:4-6)

On one of numerous occasions when Jesus appeared to His disciples after the resurrection, He said, "for John baptized with water, but you will be baptized with the Holy Spirit not many days from now" (v. 5). In spite of His clarity their minds were foggy about what He intended, and their ambitions were nothing like His. His marching orders were not what they expected. They wanted to *go* but He said *wait*. (v. 4)

His words are clear, "And while staying with them he ordered them not to depart from Jerusalem, but to wait for the promise of the Father, which, he said, 'you heard from me; for John baptized with water, but you will be baptized with the Holy Spirit not many days from now'" (vv. 4-5).

After Jesus told the disciples to expect a baptism "with the Holy Spirit," (v. 5) they should have had at least a working hunch of what was coming. After all, some of them had been disciples of John the Baptist and had, perhaps, been baptized by him in the days before they met Jesus (John 1:35-40). Jesus Himself led them to baptize disciples during the roughly three years they had been with Him (John 3:22-23; 4:1-2). They should have understood that a baptism in the Holy Spirit was in some way like the water baptism of both John and Jesus—something from God that would drench their lives!

They also should have known a lot about the person of the Holy Spirit and how powerful He is. After all, He is mentioned in the second verse of the Bible as God's powerful, personal agent of creation (Gen. 1:2).

But, all of that seemed lost on the disciples, since their thoughts were on a political renaissance for Jerusalem, including a return to the golden eras of Israel's past and a life free from Roman domination. When they heard the word *power*, all they could think to ask was, "Lord, will you at this time restore the kingdom to Israel?" (Acts 1:6).

In one sense, their provincial assumptions are not dissimilar to our own. They were mostly interested in local politics and political leverage over their perceived opponents. In these regards, they demonstrated their confusion and proved why they weren't ready to carry the message of Jesus to the world. Their focus was limited to Jerusalem, but Jesus was preparing to send them to the ends of the earth.

Promised Power (1:6-9)

In spite of the disciples' lack of comprehension about the Holy Spirit, Jesus insisted they would receive the powerful gift of the Father soon. Fortunately, His promise was not based on their understanding of the details. "So when they had come together, they asked him, 'Lord, will you at this time restore the kingdom to Israel?'" His correction was direct, but secondary to His promise. "'It is not for you to know times or seasons that the Father has fixed by his own authority. But you will receive power when the Holy Spirit has come upon you, and you will be my witnesses in Jerusalem and in all Judea and Samaria, and to the end of the earth'" (vv. 6-9).

The word "power" in verse 8 is the Greek word *dunamis*, from which we derive our English words *dynamic, dynamo,* and *dynamite*. The word means "to have the ability, strength, or power to get things done." It is interesting to note that *power* was the one thing the disciples did not have. But that was about to change, and the world would never be the same.

Power For What? (Acts 1:8)

The Holy Spirit ministered in a variety of ways in the New Testament. Jesus was conceived in the virgin's womb by the power of the Spirit (Matt.1:18). The Spirit produces godly character, called "the fruit of the Spirit," in the lives of believers (Gal. 5:22). The Holy Spirit inspired the writing of the New Testament (John 16:12-13). The Holy Spirit helps us pray (Rom. 8:26). The list of ministries the Holy Spirit accomplishes is long, and without the Holy Spirit the New Testament church would not survive. In fact, it would not exist.

Given the fact the Holy Spirit plays multiple, indispens-able roles in the life of the church, it is significant Jesus placed world evangelization at the top of the list (Acts 1:8). Jesus did not suggest the Spirit has no other ministry in the believer's life, but He only mentioned one thing: evangelism. "But you will receive power when the Holy Spirit has come upon you, and you will be my witnesses in Jerusalem and in all Judea and Samaria, and to the end of the earth." Jesus did not tell them at the time how the Holy Spirit would empower them, but the result would be evident. The disciples would become His *witnesses*.

The word "witnesses" is the Greek word *martus*. We get the English word *martyr* from it. The apostles would not have seen Jesus' use of the word martus as a cryptic hint about how their lives would end. The word became synonymous with those who were willing to die for their beliefs, but that was not the original idea. The word appears to have been derived from an old Greek word meaning *to remember*.[2] It has its history in the ancient Greek judicial system where witnesses were asked to recall what they knew, had heard, had personally experienced, or had seen. Jesus was using the word in that way. The apostles were responsible to tell what they knew about Jesus.

Jesus' ministry was meant to continue through the testimony of His witnesses, yet it was more than their physical proximity to His ministry that would qualify them for action. The fact they had traveled with Jesus, observed His ministry firsthand, and had personally seen Him after His resurrection would seem to us to be a colossal advantage in retelling His story. Yet, in spite of all of these favorable circumstances, more was required of a witness. They needed the power of the Holy Spirit.

If they needed the Spirit's immeasurable power, what do the disciples of Jesus need today? Can we expect to operate

---

[2] Gerhard Kittel, ed., *Theological Dictionary of the New Testament,* Vol IV, trans. Geoffrey W. Bromiley, (Grand Rapids, MI: Wm. B. Eerdmans Publishing Company, 1967), 475.

a worldwide missions endeavor (or for that matter, an evangelistic conversation across the street) with less power than was demanded of those original followers? We have the same story to tell today. We must be more desperate than ever to have the power that changes lives. We must rely upon the power of the Holy Spirit.

Power For A Global Outreach (Acts 1:8)

The world in Jesus' time seemed much *bigger* and unknown than it is today. Ships carried commercial or military cargo from port to port, but Jews were, for the most part, not a seafaring people. They actually feared the sea, and one aspect of their view of Heaven is that "the sea was no more" (Rev. 21:1). Therefore, international travel was mostly limited to business dealings with other Jewish communities (James 4:13). Not only that, Jews were forbidden to associate with Gentiles, even if they lived nearby. Given their natural hesitations about travel, and their systemic distrust of the non-Jewish world, why would they bother traveling among the nations? Most first century Jews, like the disciples, were content to wait for the Messianic Age when He would "restore the kingdom to Israel" (Acts 1:6).

But, the resurrection of Christ and the promise of the Holy Spirit would change everything. He told the apostles plainly, "But you will receive power when the Holy Spirit has come upon you, and you will be my witnesses in Jerusalem and in all Judea and Samaria, and to the end of the earth". The church, then and now, is called to an urgent, international mission. "You will be my witnesses in Jerusalem and in all Judea and Samaria, and to the end of the earth" (v. 8).

Jesus and His first followers had lived most of their lives in close proximity to the Sea of Galilee in the north, venturing occasionally to Jerusalem in the south. They were all working-class Jews, mostly from towns and villages not far from each other. To those small-town disciples, almost every aspect of Jesus' four-part mandate must have seemed beyond the realm of probability. For example, they were to start in Jerusalem—the same city where forty days earlier the religious authorities and the most powerful government on earth had conspired to execute Jesus. Jesus sent them there first. "All Judea," the second part of the mission, is the broader region around Jerusalem, including the unforgiving barrenness of the Judean Desert where nomadic desert-dwellers lived. Samaria, the third area, was the region populated by a people group the Jews avoided at all costs (John 4:9). But Jesus sent His disciples there too. Finally, Jesus sent a group with no political connections, no money, limited academic training, and no experience with travel to the nations of the world! No wonder they needed the Holy Spirit.

Can we see why the church has always needed and must still rely upon the Holy Spirit's unlimited power? Our world today is even more dangerous, massively more populous, and in some sectors, hardened against the gospel like never before. Jesus' words about taking the message "to the ends of the earth" force us to recognize the importance of the message and the urgency of the hour in which we live.

WHAT NEXT?

The church today must be a Spirit-filled, Spirit-empowered evangelistic and missionary force or we will have failed in the mission our Lord left us to accomplish. A study of the book of Acts will demonstrate that we are now living in the age of the Spirit's influence. For instance, in the four gospels the Spirit is mentioned directly a combined total of about fifty times. Yet in the book of Acts (approximately the length of either Matthew or Luke) we find no fewer than fifty-six direct references to the Holy Spirit, making the ministry of the Spirit one of the major themes of the book! Viewed from a slightly different perspective further highlights Luke's emphasis on the Spirit's ministry. The number of references to the Spirit in Matthew, Mark, and John total about thirty-four, while Luke's two volumes contain at least seventy-two direct references!

Today we may sense the urgency of the mission, and yet still harbor doubts about our ability to do the job. But the early church, with all of its limitations and none of our advantages, successfully evangelized most of the world they knew in a single generation. How? They were Spirit-empowered. What could we do today if we were determined to fulfill the mission in the power of the Holy Spirit—the power that changes everything?

Chapter 2
Can a Prayer Meeting Change the World?

Acts 1:12—2:13

My grandmother was a self-taught artist living on a farm during the Great Depression. She painted an impressive collection of oils that never hung in a gallery but demonstrated an original style and instinctive talent that skillfully captured rural life as she saw it. She was a natural. Even she had no idea how she taught herself to mix oils into natural shades, produce paintings on large canvases with realistic scenes, and create original art. Late in life her husband decided he would also take up painting as a pastime. Being generous in describing them, his best efforts began and ended with uninspired paint-by-number sets. She proudly showed them to the family, but the difference between original art and paint-by-number is obvious to anyone.

The stark differences between something original and dynamic versus that which is dull and predictable extend beyond a critique of amateur artwork. When we pull back the veil of excuses, the differences between the early church and its modern counterpart can be even more dramatic. Anyone who reads the book of Acts, for instance, is confronted with the stunning differences between the powerful, sweeping, spiritual actions that seemed almost commonplace in the life of the early church, compared to that which is too often inactive, ineffective, and blandly common in our own experience. These disciples seemed to live in a continuation of the ministry of Jesus. We often do not. Even apart from the occurrences of miracles, when we read the Acts narrative we sense at least two other significant differences between their church and ours.

The first distinction is the impact of the infant church on the culture around them, compared to the church's precipitous decline as a game changer in culture today. The second difference is the relentless evangelistic and spiritual zeal so typical of the early followers of Christ, compared to the virtual flat affect of so many Christians, represented in much of North America today. What happened between then and now? A more pressing question must be: is there anything we can do to recapture the dynamic life of the early church? The answer may be hidden in plain sight. We have to find it.

TRACING OUR SPIRITUAL ROOTS (Acts 1:12-14)

After the dramatic event on the Mount of Olives when Jesus physically and visibly ascended back to Heaven (vv. 9-11), the disciples made their way back up to the old city of Jerusalem, about three quarters of a mile away, to consider the phenomenon they had just seen and heard. Once inside the gates of the city they congregated in an *upper room* (v.13). In at least one other place in Scripture an important event occurred in an upper room in Jerusalem. Jesus held His final

Passover meal with the disciples in a large, furnished space designated as an upper room, donated for that purpose by an unnamed disciple who presumably lived in the city (Luke 22:12). It seems likely; the place was the same and became the meeting place for the early church.

An upper room in Jewish life was often on the flat roof of the home and could be used as a place to eat, rest, and pray. Peter took advantage of an upper room in Joppa and accomplished all three purposes (Acts 10:9-16). These rooms were spacious and usually accessible from an outside staircase.

The upper room in Acts 1:13 became one of the main places of prayer for the early church and the place where the Spirit was poured out. Because of what happened there, the upper room holds a dear place in the Christian imagination. Frequently today, and for good reason, the upper room has become nearly synonymous in the devotional vocabulary of the church as a place of communion with God. Discovering our own personal upper room is the first step in recovering our lost power and passion.

In describing the upper room prayer meeting, Luke sets the stage like a journalist with breaking news by using a few succinct statements to report, how and why the early church was powerful: "And when they had entered, they went up to the upper room, where they were staying, Peter and John and James and Andrew, Philip and Thomas, Bartholomew and Matthew, James the son of Alphaeus and Simon the Zealot and Judas the son of James. All these with one accord were devoting themselves to prayer, together with the women and Mary the mother of Jesus, and his brothers" (vv. 13-14).

As believers, our spiritual heritage is gathered in that upper room prayer meeting. The Lord's family was there (the last reference to Mary in the New Testament) along with the apostles who followed Jesus of Nazareth, led the early church, and wrote much of the New Testament. A few others are mentioned, a fairly large total assembly of 120 people (v.15). Their purpose was clear. They prayed. The last time Jesus called them to prayer on the Mount of Olives they fell asleep (Luke 22:39-46), but after what they had just witnessed on that same mountain, this time they appeared wide awake and ready to pray!

The surging influence of the early church that went on to change the world was birthed in that upper room prayer meeting. If we dig deep enough into their example and do what they did, could the fire that fell on them ignite us too? In the two thousand years since the first prayer meeting in the upper room, what have we found that has superseded it? What has God pressed us to try that has bested prayer? Perhaps we should return to the blueprint of the house of prayer.

WHY PRAYER? (1:13-14)

The disciples weren't merely *grasping at straws,* wondering what to do next, when they convened the first prayer meeting. They were following instructions. Luke's first volume details Jesus' message to the disciples in one of their last meetings with Him after the resurrection.

"Then he opened their minds to understand the Scriptures, and said to them, 'Thus it is written, that the Christ should suffer and on the third day rise from the dead, and that repentance and forgiveness of sins should be proclaimed in his name to all nations, beginning from Jerusalem. You are witnesses of these things. And behold, I am sending the promise of my Father upon you. But stay in the city until you are clothed with power from on high" (Luke 24:45-49). When coupled with similar statements in Acts 1:4-8, two things become clear. First, Luke strategically linked the last words of his first book with the first words of his second book to demonstrate the importance of Jesus' final instructions. For Luke, the evangelistic mission of the church was the reason the Spirit baptized the church with power (Luke 24:48-49; Acts 1:8). Therefore, in order to receive the Spirit's necessary power for the continuing mission of Jesus, the early church needed to wait in the city of Jerusalem for the Spirit's outpouring (Luke 24:49; Acts 1:4-5).

The second clarifying point, specifically mentioned in both Luke and Acts, relates to how the disciples interpreted the meaning of the *waiting* period. In other words, how they waited is significant. In both books the disciples understood Jesus' command to wait as a call to prayer. In Luke's last statement in his gospel, he closes with a description of the waiting of the early church, "And they worshiped him and returned to Jerusalem with great joy, and were continually in the temple blessing God." (Luke 24:52-53) In Acts, he describes them *waiting* in the upper room this way; "All these with one accord were devoting themselves to prayer..." (Acts 1:14). So, we have a composite picture of the disciples as they *waited*. They spent all their time praising God in group prayer in the temple and praying as a group in the upper room. Obviously Luke regarded the prayer meetings as the one essential activity commanded by Jesus and practiced by the early church in preparation for the outpouring of the Holy Spirit. Jesus said "wait" and they waited with unceasing prayer. The question before the contemporary reader is intriguing: would unceasing prayer in the congregation instigate similar history-making, world-changing, evangelistic results today?

PEOPLE WHO PRAY CHANGE THE WORLD (1:13-14)
Most students of Scripture are aware of the kind of people Jesus recruited to change the world. In the original team there were no trained rabbis, priests, or scribes. Instead, according to one account, they were, "uneducated, common men" (4:13). They were the fishermen, tax collectors, and others whom we met in the Gospels. "And when they had entered, they went up to the upper room, where they were staying, Peter and John and James and Andrew, Philip and Thomas, Bartholomew and Matthew, James the son of Alphaeus and Simon the Zealot and Judas the son of James" (1:13).

The core group of people we find in that first prayer meeting were fairly ordinary. So how did they change the world? The answer is so strikingly simple we almost dismiss it as secondary when in fact it is the key to understanding their effectiveness. They prayed.

They prayed together for days without ceasing. Jesus said "wait," so they prayed with expectancy, believing Jesus would make good on His promise at some point to empower them. Not knowing when or exactly how the power would come, they just kept praying.

It must also be pointed out there appears to have been no hierarchy in the prayer meeting. Apostles, unnamed others, and the family members of Jesus were all there praying. Both men and women prayed. Prayer was, and remains, the great equalizer in the church and is the ministry of everyone in the church. Every believer is called to pray (vv. 13-14). People who pray as the early church prayed always shake things up.

THE PERSISTENCE OF WORLD-CHANGING PRAYER (1:14)

For believers in the early church prayer was not a last resort: it was their first response. Luke presents a people in the upper room who made prayer the main business of their lives. "All these with one accord were devoting themselves to prayer, together with the women and Mary the mother of Jesus, and his brothers" (v. 14). Two phrases leap from the biblical page to describe the passion of that first prayer meeting.

Congregational Prayer

We are informed, "All these with one accord were devoting themselves to prayer." The word *all* is the biggest little word in the New Testament. No one opted out of the prayer meeting. Everyone was a prayer warrior in the early church! Notice, too, they were praying "with one accord." This is a unique word because, of its twelve occurrences in the New Testament, ten of them are found in the book of Acts! Their prayer meeting is a model of praying we must imitate—they were unified as if they were one person. The phrase *one accord* is only one word in the Greek New Testament but is made up of two common words: *homou*, which means "the same," and *thumos*, which means "to have strong passion." Its root word means "to breathe hard," like an athlete who has just run her fastest race. It's a word which describes the deepest feelings possible which lead to all-out effort. So, "one accord" literally means "to rush forward as the same one." It describes a unity of passion. They were together in prayer. When entire congregations decide together that prayer is their greatest resource, those churches will not stay the same for long. There are numerous examples of prayer in the book of Acts but barely one or two examples where anyone prays alone. The world-changing prayer is congregational prayer.

Committed Prayer

Luke reminds us the disciples were "devoting themselves to prayer." The word *devoting* is a powerful Greek word which describes the strength to endure. It means to persistently adhere to a thing in one place at all times. The prayer meetings in the upper room and at the temple lasted night and day for ten days. The Ascension occurred forty days after the resurrection (1:3-9) and Pentecost, which means fiftieth, occurred ten days later.

Since Luke tells us they did nothing but praise God in the temple and pray in the upper room until Pentecost, we know they prayed ten days. Their devotion to prayer helps explain why they changed the world and why, by comparison, we can appear so relatively ineffective. In my early days of ministry, I heard more than one preacher say, "They prayed ten days, preached ten minutes, and saw three thousand saved. We pray ten minutes, preach ten days, and if we see three saved we call it revival." What if we did it their way instead?

WHAT NEXT?
Prayer is a major emphasis in the book of Acts, and we cannot ignore the impact the early church had on the world as a direct result of their prayer meetings. The question each congregation needs to answer is this: If we pray like they prayed, would we see the results they saw? There is only one way to find out.

Chapter 3
A Sermon Launches a Global Movement

Acts 2:1-41

A friend of mine is a political pollster. A few years ago he offered me the opportunity to include a question on a statewide poll. I wanted to know if people had ever been significantly affected or motivated to some action by a sermon. To my pleasant surprise the vast majority of people surveyed said, "Yes." People still listen to and are motivated by the preaching of the Word.

The book of Acts contains an unusual number of sermons and speeches. There are twenty-four in all. Luke uses the speeches and sermons as a literary vehicle to help tell the story of the early church.

The fast-paced narrative of Acts is almost always centered on the movements, exploits, miraculous occurrences, missionary travels, and often dangerous adventures of the early church. But the speeches and sermons, which comprise about one third of the book, reveal carefully considered theological content woven inextricably throughout the exciting actions of the Acts storyline.[3] Of the twenty-four sermons

---

[3] John B. Polhill, *Acts*, The New American Commentary, vol. 26 (Nashville: Broadman Press, 1992), 20.

or speeches, eight are delivered by the Apostle Peter, nine by the Apostle Paul, with seven more delivered by various others.[4] Of the group, the first one is the most unforgettable.

THE CHURCH'S INAUGURAL ADDRESS (2:1-4)

The sermon delivered on the day of Pentecost was not only the first sermon in Acts, it was the first sermon of the early church! It stands as a model for the preaching that occurs frequently throughout the rest of the book.

Elements present in the other sermons draw heavily from the blueprint of Peter's sermon in Acts 2. For instance, most of the earliest sermons contained a prophetic announcement that a *new age* had dawned in which Old Testament prophecies had been, or were being, fulfilled. The ministry, death, and resurrection of Jesus of Nazareth found their way to the center of apostolic sermons. In addition, the apostles' preaching concerning Jesus of Nazareth was grounded in the Old Testament prophecies regarding the Messiah. The apostles were more than teachers merely content with dispensing religious information. They were evangelists who regarded their message as life-changing and urgent. As a result, apostolic preaching demanded a response.[5]

Could preaching today follow the blueprint found in the apostolic church? For instance, shouldn't we expect preach-

---

[4] Ibid., 43.
[5] F. F. Bruce, *The Book of Acts*, The New International Commentary of the New Testament (Grand Rapids, MI: William B. Eerdmans Publishing Company, 1998), 63.

ing to be firmly rooted in the promises of Scripture? Wouldn't we hope for preaching that focuses on the miraculous life, vicarious death, and bodily resurrection of Jesus? Aren't we expecting preaching that shows us how Jesus is our Messiah and our salvation? Couldn't preaching today be improved if every message called us out of our sin and into a deeper commitment of discipleship? If their sermons became our model, which of their practices could we adopt?

A SPIRIT FILLED SERMON (2:1-4)

The sermon that launched a global movement was conceived in the prayer room. One morning in Jerusalem, just before 9:00 a.m., Heaven rolled like a Pacific tsunami through the upper room, immersing the waiting disciples. They may have been suddenly startled or imagined, for a moment, a hurricane was whipping through the room because, "suddenly there came from heaven a sound like a mighty rushing wind, and it filled the entire house where they were sitting" (v. 2). Luke makes it clear from the outset that what happened that morning was the direct intervention of God. The entire event originated "from Heaven".

The Signs of the Spirit (2:2-4)

Jesus said the Spirit, like the wind, is invisible (John 3:8). In spite of being unseen, the Spirit makes a powerful impression. At Pentecost the Spirit came with unmistakable force and clear signs of His presence, "And suddenly there came from heaven a sound like a mighty rushing wind, and it filled the entire house where they were sitting. And divided tongues as of fire appeared to them and rested[a] on each one of them. And they were all filled with the Holy Spirit and began to speak in other tongues as the Spirit gave them utterance" (2:2-4).

Sound (v. 2)

On the day of Pentecost the coming of the Holy Spirit was "a sound like a mighty rushing wind." It was the sound, rather than the sight, of the Spirit that was like the wind. The phrase "mighty rushing wind" suggests a powerful blast. The word *mighty* is correctly translated in other translations using the English word *violent*. The word *rushing* was used by Greek seafarers to describe the propulsion of a ship when the sails were high and the winds glided the big ships across ancient seas. It doesn't take much imagination to put oneself in the place of the disciples that morning, when their prayers were interrupted by the deafening, blaring roar of what could be compared to the whirling vortex of a tornado (v. 2).

Fire (v. 3)

The second sign of the Spirit's outpouring was visible, unprecedented, and strange. Nothing quite like it had ever occurred before. Luke depicts "tongues as of fire" cascading from heaven, suddenly separating, and individually targeting each person present.

The description of the "tongues as of fire" pouring out of heaven is as vividly dramatic as it is immediately unsettling. Put yourself in their situation. What would your first reaction be if, while in a prayer meeting, incendiary blasts of flame were bursting from the ceiling and landing on the people gathered in the room? It is a breathtaking scene with no correlatives in the New Testament.

Why did the Spirit manifest as fire? While presented in a unique way at Pentecost, fire is nevertheless a frequent scriptural picture of God's presence. Richard N. Longenecker reminds us, for instance, God was present in the fire of the burning bush (Ex. 3:2-5), the pillar of fire that guided Israel by night (Ex. 13:21), and represented God's glory atop Mount Sinai (Ex. 24:17).[6] In the New Testament, John the Baptist "explicitly linked the coming of the Spirit with fire" (cf. Matt. 3:11; Luke 3:16; Acts 2:3."[7]

Speech (v. 4)

The final sign of the Spirit's coming was spiritually empowered speech. The eruption of "other tongues as the Spirit gave them utterance" was the only one of the three signs which occurred after they were filled with the Spirit. It was this sign which allowed the miraculous delivery of the first sermon. The Spirit gave them the ability to speak with supernatural power. In fact, they could not help but speak—

---

[6] Richard N. Longenecker, *Acts*, Vol. 9 of The Expositor's Bible Commentary (Grand Rapids, MI: The Zondervan Corp., 1981), 270.
[7] Ibid., 270.

the words virtually exploded out of them in a way they had never experienced before. Luke says, "as the Spirit gave them utterance."

The Greek word translated *utterance* is used only three times in the New Testament—only in Acts, and only in relation to preaching (2:4; 2:14; 26:25). It is clear in verse 4 the utterance was a miracle of "other tongues," but the emphasis is not on an ecstatic, unknown language but rather on previously unlearned, yet recognizable, language supernaturally given for preaching to a diverse audience, representing multiple languages groups (2:6,11).

Nowhere else among the other twenty-three sermons and speeches in Acts do we find the sound of the rushing wind, the tongues of fire, or other tongues. Obviously Luke did not intend to suggest that the three miraculous signs preceding the first sermon are an exact formula for the preparation of every sermon. Yet a review of each of the Apostle Peter's sermons to non-Christian audiences reveals striking similarities to the spiritual events which preceded the message at Pentecost. In every instance, his other sermons are either associated with the disciples' habit of continual prayer or they follow a miracle, a fresh infilling of the Holy Spirit, or some combination of the above (3:1-26; 4:8-12; 5:12-32; 10:19-44).

Does the sermon at Pentecost, along with the other evangelistic sermons preached by the Apostle Peter, suggest anything to us today about communicating the gospel? Does God intend for us to see a pattern we can emulate?

PROCLAIMING THE MESSAGE TODAY

While Luke's report about the Spirit's activity is not intended as a preaching textbook, there are, nonetheless, a few helpful implications to be considered. For instance, it is obvious in Acts (as well as the rest of the New Testament) the Gospel is to be communicated. It is *good news* and it is meant to be shared.

Throughout the book of Acts, speaking the Word is the primary method of spreading the Gospel of Jesus. Communication by the early church, however, was not always in a congregational or group setting. The Deacon Phillip, for example, was effective at sharing the gospel in a one-on-one encounter with a Gentile, following the leadership of the Holy Spirit (8:26-40). We discover from Phillip's example how the sermons and speeches can be a pattern not only for preachers but by all other believers who desire to share their faith.

Spiritual Preparations

The first proclamations of the gospel were initiated in a prayer meeting. Why would we ever hope to experience the kind of power they experienced if we won't prepare in prayer? Likewise, the first proclamations were Spirit-led from their inception. No sermon manufactured by human ingenuity can hope to compare to a message blazing to life from the furnace of the Spirit's fiery presence. Our witness should reflect the supernatural presence of divine anointing if we want to see God move in our culture as He moved in theirs.

Biblical Sermons (2:16-36)

The life, death, and resurrection of Jesus were central elements in the early sermons of the church. One surprising aspect of apostolic preaching is the overwhelming absence of references concerning their own experiences with Jesus which the apostles might have understandably been tempted to include. Instead, the first sermon was a biblical exposition from Old Testament texts pointing to the death and resurrection of Christ and the present ministry of the Holy Spirit.

Peter began with an explanation of Joel 2:28-32 to demonstrate the fulfillment of prophecy related to the Spirit's work in the "last days" (Acts 2:17-21). He also explained the meaning of the resurrection of Christ from Psalm 16:8-11 (Acts 2:25-28). Peter then proclaimed the ascension of Christ, His exaltation as the anticipated Jewish Messiah, and the fact He is Lord of all, from Psalm 110:1 (Acts 2:32-36). Of the twenty-seven verses of Peter's sermon, ten of the verses, or 37 percent, are direct quotations of the Old Testament. The earliest proclamation of the church was a clearly and deliberately a *biblical sermon*.

In our culture of personal experience, which often dismisses the value of absolute truth, there has never been a better time to follow the example of the first sermon and base our witness on Scripture. We may justifiably illustrate the Scripture from our personal experience but the message is strongest when we proclaim the Bible.

A Call to Action (2:36-41)

Peter was not content to stop at proclamation—he was preaching for persuasion. The decisive moment in the message was Peter's insistence that his hearers were personally responsible for the crucifixion. His words were like javelins piercing their hearts. The word used to describe the "cut" into their consciences is a strong word used nowhere else in the New Testament. The root word, however, is the same as the one used to describe the soldier's action with a spear when he "pierced" Jesus' side as He hung upon the cross (John 19:34).

It is difficult to imagine how much more direct Peter could have been in declaring their guilt, "Let all the house of Israel therefore know for certain that God has made him both Lord and Christ, this Jesus whom you crucified. Now when they heard this they were cut to the heart, and said to Peter and the rest of the apostles, 'Brothers, what shall we do'" (Acts 2:36-37).

They understood the message, they were convicted of sin, and they desired to respond. Peter advised them to repent and be baptized (v. 38). That day, as a result, three thousand people were baptized and the church was born. It was a day that changed the world.

CONCLUSION

Not every Christian is a *preacher* in the typical sense, but every believer is responsible for communicating the message of the gospel to the unbelieving world. The pattern established by the first sermon suggests our gospel presentations should flow out of our persistent prayer lives. In addition, we should trust in the supernatural power of the Holy Spirit who draws and convinces those who hear us. We should confidently communicate Scripture, which has the raw power to change lives, and we should be unapologetic in a calling for a response to the Gospel.

After two thousand years few, if any, sermons have been preached with results equal to the message at Pentecost. Yet we can still expect life-changing results since we can proclaim the same message. Perhaps most importantly, the Holy Spirit is still at work today, just as He was when a single sermon launched a global movement which continues to change the world.

Chapter 4
The Church the Holy Spirit Builds

Acts 2:41-47

At the highest point in the city of London, towering almost four hundred feet, stands one of the most celebrated churches in the world. St. Paul's Cathedral, the eighteenth century architectural masterpiece of Sir Christopher Wren, has been a silent witness to some of the most famous events in recent British history. The funerals of British Prime Ministers Winston Churchill and Margaret Thatcher, as well as the wedding of Prince Charles and Lady Diana, were both solemn and ceremonial events watched on television around the world. Sir Christopher Wren himself is buried in the crypt of the church beneath a plaque which reads, in part, "Reader, if you seek his monument—look around you."

A visit to London would be incomplete without seeing St. Paul's. It is a tribute to the architect and to the determination of the city. The church was rebuilt after the Great Fire of London. Eighteen hundred years earlier, following the fire of Pentecost, the Holy Spirit built a church too. But it is far more impressive than the English baroque design of St. Paul's, even though the Spirit's church has no great dome, no towers, and no carved stone. In fact, the first church wasn't a building at all.

When the Holy Spirit brought the first church to life, the physical surroundings were of little importance. The dynamic church grew exponentially while meeting in the Jewish temple courts and in local homes. Yet, in spite of its humble real estate holdings, the early church spread the message of Jesus through the Roman Empire in a single generation. Instead of physical advantages, the early church had spiritual life pulsing through its veins.

OUR FAMILY ALBUM (2:37-42)

From the opening verses of Acts, events full of astonishing and miraculous activity unfold. Jesus is raised to life and physically, visibly ascends into the clouds with angels standing nearby promising His return. Tongues of fire fall from heaven while the roar of a whirlwind fills the house where the disciples are praying.

Thousands of people respond to the church's first sermon, and in one day they immerse three thousand people in baptism. Then, as if the action is suddenly slowed to allow reflection on what has transpired, Luke offers a summary—a kind of *snapshot*—of life as it was in the early church. "So those who received his word were baptized, and there were added that day about three thousand souls. And they devoted themselves to the apostles' teaching and the fellowship, to the breaking of bread and the prayers" (2:41-42).

OBEYING THE GREAT COMMISSION (2:41-42)

When Jesus left the work of His kingdom to the apostles' care, He instructed them to, "Go therefore and make disciples of all nations, baptizing them in the name of the Father and of the Son and of the Holy Spirit, teaching them to observe all that I have commanded you. And behold, I am with you always, to the end of the age" (Matt. 28:19-20). Jesus had instructed His followers to do three things: make disciples, baptize the new disciples, and teach the newly baptized disciples. When the apostles had their first opportunity, they followed His instructions perfectly.

Make Disciples (v. 41)

In the New Testament disciples are learners who have accepted the teaching of a rabbi, teacher, or leader. For every disciple there must be a beginning point—a first step of believing and following. At Pentecost three thousand people became newborn disciples when they believed Peter's message about Jesus. "So those who received his word were baptized, and there were added that day about three thousand souls." (2:41).

Baptize Them (v. 41)

The word *baptism* (or some form of it) is common in the book of Acts and throughout the New Testament. The Greek root word *baptizo* occurs more than one hundred times in at least nine books, but is found predominately in the Gospels and

Acts. It means "to immerse or submerge." Jesus left explicit instructions that new followers were to be baptized after their conversion (Matt. 28:19). Peter's sermon led to three thousand baptisms in one day.

They were baptized in stone pools, called *mikvahs*, capable of holding hundreds of gallons of water each. Pre-Christian era Jews used the mikvahs to purify themselves by immersion prior to entering the temple. These ancient baptismal pools were common in the time of Jesus and are still visible in Jerusalem today, outside the Temple Mount.

Imagine the excitement and witness of three thousand people being baptized as new followers of Jesus, a little less than two months after He had been crucified! Baptism demonstrated then, and it demonstrates now, the community of Jesus is alive and well.

Teach Them (v. 42)

Immediately after the mass baptism, the apostles gathered the new believers into a community for teaching and growth. Luke describes the new church as an extension of the apostles' own experience under the rabbinical tutelage of Jesus. "And they devoted themselves to the apostles' teaching and the fellowship, to the breaking of bread and the prayers" (2:42). The summary Luke provides in verse 42 is intended to be seen as idyllic. This is the church the Holy Spirit built—it was thoroughly evangelical and intentional about discipleship.

The apostles had followed the Great Commission verbatim. They made disciples (v. 41), they baptized them (v. 41), and they taught them (v. 42). This picture of the evangelistic, disciple-making church is a glimpse of the church at its finest.

THE DEVOTED CHURCH (2:42)

One night after a special evangelistic service at a church in Stone Mountain, Georgia, a young man spoke to his pastor about recommitting his life to Christ. His exact words are unforgettable, "This low-grade-temperature Christianity is killing me!" He was on to something. Living without passion is colorless and empty. The Christian life was meant for more than that. The earliest church was the opposite of dispassionate and cool. They were red-hot with devotion.

Luke's summary of the church after Pentecost describes the zeal of the early Christians. "And they devoted themselves to the apostles' teaching and the fellowship, to the breaking of bread and the prayers" (v. 42).

The word *devoted* comes from a combination of two Greek words. The first means "toward" or "forward." The second part of the word means "to exercise continuous strength." The literal idea is *to lean forward into a thing with persistent strength*. In other words, being devoted means being passionately committed and wholehearted in persistence.

God desires devotion, produced by the Spirit, in the lives of those who follow Jesus. He wanted it then and He wants it now.

Details of Devotion (Acts 2:42)

We might wish we had more details about the exciting days of the early church. Three thousand people is a big group. How did they manage all the people? Many of them were from out of town. Did they relocate to Jerusalem or leave after a short time to go home? Questions of that nature seem secondary to Luke who isn't interested in those details. Instead, he focuses on the details related to God's eternal purpose for the church.

Apostles' Teaching (v.42)

Although he doesn't offer us a class schedule or a syllabus, Luke presents the early church as a passionate learning environment where "they devoted themselves to the apostles teaching". Since they focused on "the apostles' teaching," we can deduce two things. The short phrase "apostles' teaching" describes both who was teaching and what was taught. The apostles, as the teachers, taught what they had learned from their three-year association with Jesus, and the insight gained from Him during the forty days after the resurrection when He devoted His time "speaking about the kingdom of God" (1:3).

The "apostles' teaching" in those early sessions forms the basis of our New Testament. The *professors* of the apostolic *seminary* were Matthew, who wrote the Gospel bearing his name; John, who wrote five New Testament books; and Peter, who wrote two letters and influenced Mark's writing. In addition James, Jude, and Mark were present in the early church, and all wrote books found in the New Testament. The only New Testament writers not present in the first *school* of the church were Paul and Luke.

The Fellowship (v. 42)

The early Christians were devoted to learning but they were also devoted to "the fellowship" (v. 42). The word *fellowship* means the community or the things shared. It describes that which is held in common. From its inception, the church was a new people-group on the earth. These believers were associated with and committed to each other like a large family or tribal group. What Israel had been in the Old Testament—the obvious, gathered people of God— the church is now. For the church, being devoted to "the fellowship" was more than a sentimental feeling of goodwill and friendship, as we tend to define fellowship today. Instead, "the fellowship" was another way of describing the uniqueness of the church's identity, separate from the rest of Judaism and the world around them.

Breaking Bread (v. 42)

The "breaking of bread" probably reflects two things. First, it describes the community's habit of eating together as a group. It portrays the church as a family. We know they ate as a group because verse 46 emphasizes the way they shared meals—in various houses around the city. There were 3,120 of them from the beginning and more were added every day (v. 47). So the habit of eating together and managing food distribution became more complex and helped create the first recorded internal struggle for the early church (6: 1-2).

In addition to simply eating together, "the breaking of bread" probably refers to the earliest expressions of the communion meal or the *Lord's Supper*. In the early days, the Communion meal may have been a part of the larger, shared meal of the group.[8] It appears the habits of eating together and the Lord's Supper were not completely separate issues until a decade or more after the birth of the early church. Paul, for example, would later confront the church at Corinth for their excessive eating and drinking, to the point of drunkenness, in the name of the Lord's Supper. Due to the excesses, Paul advised separating the Lord's Supper from other meals (1 Cor. 11:17-30). Whatever is meant by the "breaking of bread" in the Jerusalem church, Luke regards it as an essential component of church life after Pentecost.

---

[8] John R. W. Stott, *The Message of Acts,* The Bible Speaks Today (Downers Grove, IL: InterVarsity Press, 1990), 85.

The Prayers (v. 42)

The early church lived in prayer. The prayer meeting that began in the upper room (1:14) continued after the Spirit brought the church to life. The prayers, mentioned as representative of the church in Acts 2:42, appear to be more than the all-important personal, private devotions of individual Christians. Instead of *prayer*, the English Standard Version of the Bible accurately translates verse 42 as "the prayers." The prayers were both plural and have a definite article in Greek, implying prayer meetings and gatherings. Of all the prayers mentioned in the book of Acts, nearly all of them are in groups rather than examples of individuals in private prayer. The lesson for us today should be apparent. The church is most powerful and reflective of God's original design when we are in prayer meetings with other believers.

CONCLUSION

The simplicity of the early church structure may be difficult to replicate in existing churches in the modern, Western context. Complex structures are the norm, especially in older churches, but the aboriginal principles of fellowship around the Lord's table, studying the Word, building community, and ceaseless devotion to praying together hold out a potent appeal for the building up of the church. Their devotion to a church built by the Holy Spirit changed their world. Following their example of devotion may change ours.

Chapter 5
Life-changing Miracles
Acts 3–4

Miracles happen. They are an integral part of the early church narrative that unfolds in Acts. From the opening sentences of the book, when Jesus miraculously appears after His death and then visibly ascends to Heaven, we are prepared for a world where supernatural events occur.

Two distinct kinds of miracles are recorded in Acts. The first kind takes place without any human participation at all. For instance, God raised Jesus from the dead and lifted Him to heaven with no human involvement (1:3, 9). Other examples of miracles like that include the tongues of fire and the sound of the rushing winds bellowing through the prayer meeting at Pentecost (2:2-3).

On the other hand, several miracles occur because God gifted the apostles, and a few others, to exercise ministries of healing and exorcisms just the way Jesus had done (2:43; 6:8; 8:6). In those instances, God worked through the ministries of the disciples rather than independently of them. There are at least a dozen references to these types of miracles mentioned in the book of Acts (5:1-11; 9:40; 14:8-11). In addition, there are numerous references to miracles without any specific events described (2:43; 6:8; 5:12; 8:6; 14:3). An example is found in the early days of the ministry in Jerusalem when,

"...many signs and wonders were regularly done among the people by the hands of the apostles...." (5:12).

There are also demonstrations of miraculous power paralleling the most astonishing displays of Jesus' own power, including at least two examples when the apostles raised the dead (9:36-42; 20:9-12). But for all of the amazing events performed through the apostles' miraculous ministry, none requires as much space to describe as the first specific miracle mentioned— the healing of the crippled beggar at the Beautiful Gate. In a book with only twenty-eight chapters available to tell the story of the first three decades of the early church, Luke uses nearly two entire chapters to tell about one miracle and its aftermath (3:1-26; 4:1-31). Why does Luke give so much attention to one event?

THE MIRACLE (3:1-26)

Luke never misses an opportunity to show the early church in prayer. One afternoon at 3:00 p.m., Peter and John were walking toward the temple to pray when they encountered a man they may have recognized, since the man was laid at the entrance to the temple every day. He was a middle-aged man who had been born with a birth defect which prevented him from walking. The Greek word translated "lame" in verse 2 is strikingly picturesque in that it can simply mean lacking a foot. The man obviously had feet, but the word picture is telling. His feet were so useless that it would have been no different if he had none. As a result, he had been lying by the gate begging for gifts from strangers and anyone else passing by. It was a miserable way to live.

The Beautiful Gate mentioned as the location of the miracle is difficult to identify since there appears to be no extant Jewish literature from the period indicating a gate by that name. The Jewish historian, Josephus, however, was familiar with the temple and described ten gates leading into the temple's courts, and one, made of Corinthian bronze, was visibly larger and more valuable than the other nine.[9] There by that elaborate gate, the deformed man watched as healthy people went where he could not go—into the temple to worship God. One day, the unimaginable occurred and everything changed forever. Two disciples of Jesus walked by, and an unexpected miracle took place.

As Peter and John, along with a large crowd of others, were headed in to pray, the crippled man asked for alms. In Jewish life, giving money to the poor was a spiritual discipline on par with prayer and fasting (Matt. 6:1-18). Therefore, it was natural to assume if Jews were headed into the temple to pray, asking for a few coins at the moment before they entered the temple could generate a positive outcome. The response of Peter and the John was completely different than any the man had experienced before.

The disciples stopped and insisted the man look at them. They told him they had no money, but had something of greater value—the power of God to heal him. Peter spoke

---

[9] John B. Polhill, *Acts*, The New American Commentary, vol. 26 (Nashville: Broadman Press, 1992), 126-127.

"in the name of Jesus Christ of Nazareth," and told the man to "rise up and walk" (3:6). The exact combination of name and titles used by Peter, "Jesus Christ of Nazareth," leaves no doubt about the source of the divine power. The use of Jesus' name in that exact word order is found nowhere else in the New Testament except in Peter's defense of the miracle before the Jewish rulers the next day (4:10).

One thing is clear from these two passages: from the earliest days of the church, Jesus was regarded as much more than simply "Jesus of Nazareth." He is the *Christ*. Peter's addition of the designation "of Nazareth" to the name and title "Jesus Christ," meant there could be no question about which Jesus (one of the most common names in first century Judaism) was being given credit for the miracle. He is never referred to as Jesus of Nazareth again in the New Testament outside the Gospels and Acts.

The miracle was immediate. The man who had never walked jumped to his feet and started leaping with unbridled excitement. The miracle was done in a prominent location at a critical time with a large group of witnesses. Once inside the temple, the formerly crippled man, who was well known to the regular worshippers (v.16), continued to jump and praise God. He was overjoyed and impossible to ignore.

A large crowd followed Peter to Solomon's Portico, a massive area across from the Court of the Gentiles where the church frequently assembled (5:12). Peter immediately started preaching. He reminded the people of the miracle they had witnessed and invited them to repent and be saved through faith in Jesus. As always, Peter linked the ministry of

Jesus to the Old Testament prophecies concerning the Jewish Messiah as he called for the crowd to repent and believe.

The miracle of healing the crippled man isn't unique in the New Testament. In fact, it is reminiscent of similar miracles performed by Jesus and later by the Apostle Paul (Matt. 9:1-8; Mark 2:1-12; John 5:1-9; Acts 14:8-10). Since the miracle itself is not a one-of-a-kind event, there are a few apparent reasons Luke devoted so much space to telling the story of the healing.

First, this particular miracle demonstrated how the powerful ministry of Jesus was now continuing through His church. Second, Luke uses the miracle as a bridge to another *speech*, which he frequently uses to repeat the Gospel. Finally, he mentions the miracle as a way of showing how the persecution of the church began.

THE PERSECUTION BEGINS (4:1-22)
Peter's sermon was highly effective because the church in Jerusalem, as a result, increased in size to five thousand men. The larger community, including women and families, probably numbered two to three times more. Religious leaders were in shock. Caiaphas and Annas, leaders in the priesthood, had only recently dealt with Jesus. They thought they silenced Him by helping to orchestrate His crucifixion. Now His disciples are acting boldly—preaching to massive crowds, baptizing thousands of Jewish converts, and working miracles just as Jesus had done. The religious leaders were being overwhelmed by a movement they could not stop.

In fact, the more they tried to stop it the more out of their control it got. Sadly, the fact they could not stop what God was doing did not prevent them from trying.

As a result of the miracle and the sermon that followed, the rulers arrested Peter and John and detained them overnight. What followed is a display of God's amazing power working in His church.

The religious leaders had every advantage against the apostles except one. These leaders had centuries of tradition, wealth, political connections, respectable positions of authority, and the most impressive religious real estate on earth. Yet they were powerless against two fishermen from Galilee.

When the Jewish priests brought in Peter and John for interrogation they were surprised by the boldness of the two disciples. Instead of being intimidated by the council, Peter was "filled with the Holy Spirit" (4:8) and preached the gospel. As a result of that sermon, for two thousand years the church has been blessed with one of the greatest affirmations about the identity and purpose of Jesus found anywhere in the New Testament. Peter said, "And there is salvation in no one else, for there is no other name under heaven given among men by which we must be saved" (4:12).

The religious leaders were exposed in their weakness. Rather than stopping the spread of the Christian message, they recognized the disciples had the same qualities Jesus had displayed. The two men detained for questioning were ordinary men without rabbinical credentials. Instead, the disciples were empowered with the same scriptural insights and miraculous power the religious councils had feared so much in Jesus Himself!

In the face of the supernatural force so obviously at work in the disciples, the rulers were reduced to empty warnings. The healed man was standing in front of them, and to deny the miracle was impossible and ludicrous (4:16). So they warned the disciples not to preach anymore in the name of Jesus. They may as well have insisted the sun should stop shining. Peter and John recognized the rulers had no authority, and they were quick to assure them nothing could deter them from their mission (4:18-22).

The disciples had won the first round in a persecution battle that would follow them for the rest of their lives.

By telling the story of the miracle at the gate Luke accomplished at least three objectives. First, he demonstrated that the church, then and now, ministers in the power and authority of Jesus Christ. Second, he showed how a life changed by the power of Jesus is one of the church's most powerful apologetics. Finally, he revealed the origin of the hostility against the church that would soon lead to the tragic death of the first Christian martyr (ch. 7). By showing us the source of the persecution, which would incite religious leaders to kill Christians, Luke subtly prepares us to meet a man who hated everything about the church and would become its most violent opponent (chs. 8–9).

THE PRAYING CHURCH DOES IT AGAIN (4:23-31)

In spite of the amount of space devoted to the story of the miracle, Luke isn't finished. The story begins with the apostles *headed to* a prayer meeting, and the story concludes with the apostles *in* a prayer meeting!

Luke's interest in prayer is unparalleled by the other writers who shared in the responsibility of archiving the history of Christianity's origins. It's tempting to wonder if prayer was completely foreign to Luke's experience before he became a follower of Christ because he lived the rest of his life overwhelmed by the power of prayer. Luke portrays the early church in a consistent light; they prayed about everything.

As soon as they had been released, the apostles went immediately to the prayer meeting (4:23). The church appealed to a power greater than the power of the religious leaders. They didn't ask for an easier environment in which to minister. On the contrary, they found biblical evidence confirming the reason for the "trials" and sought God for greater boldness to preach their message in the face of growing persecution (4:24-30).

To confirm the importance of the church's prayer ministry, another miracle occurred. "And when they had prayed, the place in which they were gathered together was shaken, and they were all filled with the Holy Spirit and continued to speak the word of God with boldness" (4:31).

Yes, the apostles performed incredible miracles, but behind their public preaching and spectacular signs was the kneeling form of a praying church filled with the Holy Spirit. Prayer in the Spirit is the secret power that every congregation in every generation can emulate.

By concluding the story of the miracle with a visit to the *prayer room*, Luke reminds us, when the church prays, God still answers with power and miracles still happen.

Chapter 6
A Faith Worth Dying For
Acts 6–7

Christian persecution is real. We have all observed the horrific news stories about Christians tortured and beheaded, detained as hostages; children killed in front of Christian parents who refuse to deny Jesus, and other acts of brutality beyond our comprehension. One veteran missionary and author has documented persecution and Christian martyrdom escalating around the world. He recently wrote, "A new Jesus movement is erupting around the world, and persecuted believers are leading the way."[10]

Martyrdom for the cause of Christ is real, but it is not new. It did not begin with jihad or as part of a twenty-first century philosophy of global terrorism. Christian martyrdom began where the church began, in Jerusalem, not far from the place where Jesus was raised from the dead. From the very beginning, Christianity was a faith worth dying for.

THE FIRST CHRISTIAN MARTYR (6:1-8)
Stephen was the first person in history to die for his faith in Jesus. He was an outstanding example of faith in the early

---

[10] Tom Doyle with Greg Webster, *Killing Christians*, (Nashville: W Publishing Group, 2015), xiii.

church. When the apostles urged the church in Jerusalem to identify a group of Spirit-filled men, full of wisdom and of great reputation in the church, Stephen was the first man chosen (vv. 3-5). His faith was evident, and the church knew they could trust him (v. 5).

In addition to the daily administrative work the church assigned to Stephen and a few others, he was a persistent evangelistic preacher. He was so persuasive it seemed as if no one could successfully dispute him in the exchange of ideas. God had gifted him as an able administrator, a powerful evangelist, a man of faith, and a spiritually wise leader. But there was more. God worked miracles through Stephen's ministry that Luke called "great wonders and signs" (vv. 8-10).

In the book of Acts, until the ministry of Stephen, only the apostles of Jesus had been able to perform "wonders and signs." In fact, signs and wonders were so rare outside of the apostles' ministry; Stephen was one of only three other men who performed miracles in Acts. Stephen's fellow-deacon, Phillip the Evangelist, performed miracles, and so did Barnabas as long as he was with Paul (8:6; 14:3; 15:12). The reason these three men were singled out for this additional power is not explicitly stated, however, there is one obvious similarity. Each of these disciples was a groundbreaker in taking the gospel to the Gentile world.

Stephen, for instance, spoke of the Jewish temple as an insufficient house for the God of creation (7:48-49), implying God has the power and freedom to call others outside of Judaism to Himself, as He had done by calling Abraham out of paganism in the first place (7:2-4). In addition, Stephen's martyrdom is the transitional event that drove the Christian church out of Jerusalem and into other parts of Israel, and eventually to the Gentiles throughout the Roman Empire (8:1-2). Paul, the missionary to the Gentiles, is introduced in the Stephen story, and Paul's conversion would be instrumental in taking Christianity to the rest of the world.

Phillip was gifted to perform miracles, and as a result of the persecution in Jerusalem following Stephen's martyrdom, he was the first person to take the gospel to the Samaritans (8:4-25). In addition, Phillip was the first preacher to evangelize an Ethiopian, thus allowing the Gospel to travel to Africa (8:26-40). Finally, Barnabas traveled with Paul on the first mission trip among the Gentile world (13:46). It seems clear, therefore, the three men who were not apostles in any primary sense of the word, were unusually gifted to perform miracles because they were trailblazers who took the gospel outside of Judaism and into the wider Gentile world.

Stephen is a major figure in the story of the spread of Christianity. He remains one of the best examples of Christian devotion in history, but as a result of that devotion, his own history would be all too brief.

FAMILIAR FALSE CHARGES (6:9-15)

As a historian Luke is interested in details such as the names of the Jewish groups who first raised objections to Stephen's ministry. Little is known of them now beyond what may be deduced from their names, but they were probably known to Luke's original audience (vv. 8-10). One of the synagogues was made up of "those from Cilicia" (v. 9). It is only possible to speculate, but the mention of this group may have been Luke's subtle way of telling us how Saul of Tarsus became involved in the story of Stephen, since Tarsus was the capital city of Cilicia in modern day Turkey.

Men from the various synagogues collaborated to dispute publicly with Stephen but were helpless in the face of the grace and power of God present in Stephen's life. Unable to undermine Stephen's message, the men turned instead to lies and distortion to bring the official Jewish authorities against Stephen. They accused him of blasphemy (v.11), stirred up the public (v.12), and arranged for a group of "false witnesses" to accuse Stephen of threatening harm against the temple and Jewish customs (vv.13-14). The charges sound strikingly similar to the tactics and false charges leveled against Jesus (Matt. 26:57-66).

THE SERMON (7:1-53)

Stephen's sermon before the Sanhedrin is a retelling of Jewish history beginning with the call of Abraham in Genesis 12 to the completion and dedication of Solomon's temple. While he spoke, Stephen was under the scrutiny of the angry crowd who had instigated the trial, as well as the high priest and other leaders who had already warned Peter and John not to preach in Jesus' name (4:18). It was a tense scene.

The high priest asked only one question, "Are these things so?" (v. 1). Stephen recognized an opportunity and launched into one of the greatest extemporaneous sermons ever preached. He immediately identified himself as a Jew, like his accusers, fully knowledgeable of God's grace toward the Jewish people. His sermon is a brilliant summary of hundreds of years of Jewish history, making it clear he had more than a passing grasp of the Old Testament.

All the while as Stephen was preaching, his accusers were silent. We can only imagine the impact of Stephen's message on the consciences of his stubborn congregation. Luke even adds the detail that Stephen's face took on an angelic quality (6:15). The Sanhedrin was confronted by the glory of God resting on a man they were ready to kill. What could be more obviously contradictory? They were accusing him of blaspheming God, and yet the glory of God had settled on him in their very presence. The leaders were speechless as he effortlessly weaved his way through the Old Testament.

Suddenly, Stephen got personal, direct, and forceful. He skipped past the vast majority of the Old Testament written by the Jewish prophets. Instead, he confronted his makeshift congregation with an indictment: "Which of the prophets did your fathers not persecute? And they killed those who announced beforehand the coming of the Righteous One, whom you have now betrayed and murdered" (v. 52). Rather than simply remind the Jewish leaders about the prophets, he became like one of them. His words were pointed and intentionally inflammatory. He accused his accusers! They had charged him with changing religious customs. He accused them of murdering the Son of God. Which of those two things would be worse in the eyes of God? At that point

Stephen's death, if there had been any lingering doubt, was a certainty.

THE EXECUTION OF THE FIRST MARTYR (7:54-60)

The language of the attack against Stephen was violent. The ruling council and the accusers were outraged. The word Luke used to describe their fury literally means their hearts were torn apart as if a carpenter sawed them into pieces. Their frustration was clear. Their jaws tightened and they started to grind their teeth as if, in their anger, they had lost all control of their senses (v. 54). Stephen, however, was the opposite. He was caught up in a transcendent moment of worship. Luke returns to one of the themes of Acts as he portrays Stephen being rushed upon, screamed at, pulled in every direction, and yet filled with the Holy Spirit.

By the time Luke wrote Acts, persecution was common for every believer, and there was no end in sight. Luke's first readers, no strangers to persecution, were reminded that even during the worst forms of persecution, the Spirit will fill believers and remain with them to strengthen His church. Stephen's story was one of assurance.

As Christians experience a new wave of persecution today, Stephen's story reminds us God never abandons His people. The Holy Spirit is still capable of lifting our spirits into the presence of God at the precise moment when persecutors aim their hatred at us.

In a moment of revelation, Stephen saw Jesus "standing at the right hand of God" (v. 55). The Lord miraculously diverted Stephen's attention from the chaos and threats around him and opened his eyes to the glory of the world that awaited him.

Elsewhere Jesus is said to be "seated at the right hand" of God (Eph. 1:20; Col. 3:1; Heb. 8:1; 10:12, for example). Luke does not attempt to explain why Stephen saw Jesus standing, but the image presented is deeply moving. The Son of God rising from His throne to reveal Himself, His glory, and His concern for His martyred saint is a powerful picture of what awaits every believer when life ends. We will see Jesus, regardless of His posture, and we will be with Him at last.

Stephen seemed blissfully unaware of the mob forming around and physically dragging him to a place of execution. Instead of panic and fear, Stephen testified, "Behold, I see the heavens opened, and the Son of Man standing at the right hand of God" (v. 56). Physically, Stephen was in Jerusalem standing before his executioners, but his spirit was already being caught up to join the resurrected and glorified Lord.

In the midst of the frenzy, Luke introduces us to a young man named Saul of Tarsus (v. 58). Saul was a zealous Pharisee stirred to the core with bloodlust at the sight of Stephen's execution.

The mob, along with Saul, took Stephen to a location outside the city and stoned the preacher to death. Apparently, in order to improve the accuracy of their aim while they threw the rocks that killed Stephen, they removed their coats to free their arms from the confines of the restrictive robes. They placed the garments in front of young Saul. When Luke later focuses on Saul in more detail (8:3), he will describe him as a man motivated to repeat the murder of Stephen as often as possible in order to destroy the church. Of course, we know God had a much different plan.

In his final words, we hear an echo of Jesus in Stephen's last prayer, "And as they were stoning Stephen, he called out, 'Lord Jesus, receive my spirit.' And falling to his knees he cried out with a loud voice, 'Lord, do not hold this sin against them.' And when he had said this, he fell asleep" (7:59-60). When Jesus was dying on the cross He had said nearly the same words. Both of the sayings of Jesus are found in Luke's Gospel which indicates Luke purposefully drew attention to the similarities. The final words of the martyr, echoing his Savior, demonstrate the holiness of Stephen, while Luke's explicit comparison to the Lord's dying words may be a strong indicator of the place Stephen held in the hearts of the early church. Jesus had also prayed for His tormentors to be forgiven (Luke 23:34). His last words on the cross were also a prayer that God the Father would receive His spirit when he died (Luke 23:46). Stephen had lived for Jesus. In the end, he also died like Jesus.

STEPHEN'S LASTING LEGACY

In many ways, Stephen is one of the greatest, and simultaneously one of the most unsung heroes of the New Testament. Like John the Baptist before him, Stephen's role is primarily transitional, helping to introduce another character.

The Baptizer had introduced Jesus, and Stephen's story helps introduce Paul. Though his story impressively stands alone, he is overshadowed by the person who comes after him.

Stephen's life and death serve as a reminder that even if we lose our lives in service to the Lord, Jesus will be with us to the end. While Stephen's devotion has resonated at times of persecution through the centuries, today his life of faithfulness is an important encouragement, as martyrdom for Christ rises around the world. Like the martyrs in Revelation, Stephen is a spiritual example of those before and after us who gain the final victory, "by the blood of the Lamb and by the word of their testimony, for they loved not their lives even unto death" (Rev. 12:11).

Chapter 7
A Changed Man Can Change History

Acts 8–9

Saul of Tarsus was a terrifying enemy of the fledging Christian movement in its infancy. His eagerness to violently drag men and women out of their homes to have them imprisoned, while he advocated for their deaths, made him infamous among the young, Jewish Christian community that was already being scattered for their safety across the Middle East.

INTRODUCING SAUL OF TARSUS

Saul was a young man—probably only in his early twenties—when the Christian leader, Stephen, had been murdered. The Greek root word describing Saul's age is *neos*, from which we derive the English word "new" and the prefix "neo-" (7:58). In the Greek text the word *neos* always means young, fresh, or some word implying newness. He was at the age when athletes and ground troops are in their prime.

Saul of Tarsus was highly educated. He was the best in his class at the most coveted rabbinical school in Jerusalem, discipled personally by the leading, most brilliant, and respected pharisaical rabbi of the time. Saul was an elitist from a wealthy family of strict Jews living abroad and operating a business in one of the ancient world's most well-known cities for trade guilds and international, commercial enterprise.

His family did business in a city of the Roman Empire where Greek customs and language were still the predominate influence, left over from the days three centuries earlier when Alexander the Great had spread the Greek culture, called Hellenism, throughout the region. In that cosmopolitan city, protected by a mountain range on one side and the Mediterranean Sea which provided a constant flow of commercial trade ships to and from their ports on the other side, Saul's family had acquired their prestigious, Roman citizenship and amassed their fortune.

Saul was what we call today a *Type-A* personality. He was an *alpha male* in a culture of alpha males. He had no shortage of self-confidence, which was coupled with Jewish nationalism and unparalleled religious zeal in a day of zealots. Ambition and pride came naturally to the highly-accomplished young Saul, but after a bloodthirsty mob stoned Stephen, something seems to have snapped in the young man's mind. He had discovered a maniacal and murderous mission. He concluded he would devote himself to one cause. He would do what others before him had failed to do—he would eradicate Christianity from the face of the earth. He would do it by any means available to him and single-handedly if he had to. Saul had been radicalized.

THE INEVITABLE CONFRONTATION (8:1-9:1)

When there were no repercussions from Stephen's assassination—when the Roman authorities didn't bother to investigate or intervene, and the church began to leave town in droves as a result—Saul of Tarsus became a predator, like a carnivorous beast with an insatiable taste for blood. Luke used a word found nowhere else in the New Testament to describe Saul's vitriolic, hate-filled, and vicious actions against the church. He said, "But Saul was ravaging the church..." (8:3). The word *ravaging* describes a brutal rage and is used outside the Bible in Greek literature to describe the ferocious attack of a wild animal mauling a defenseless person.[11]

Saul was like a wolf devouring what appeared to him, at the time, to be a flock of helpless sheep. He would discover later the sheep weren't as defenseless as he imagined. Until something or someone stopped him, however, Saul's goal was nothing short of more Christians dead, as he continued to breathe the intoxicating air of newfound power, which he felt fully justified in exercising (9:1).

THE ROAD TO DAMASCUS (9:1-19)

Since the followers of Jesus had fled the city, Saul decided to pursue them. He acquired the necessary documents from the high priest, which amounted to extradition papers. Saul was

---

[11] John MacArthur, *The MacArthur Bible Commentary,* (Nashville: Nelson Reference & Electronic, A Division of Thomas Nelson Publishers, 2005) 1,450.

no longer merely a wunderkind rabbi in Jerusalem. He had become an international bounty hunter. When Saul learned believers had fled to Damascus, Syria about 135 miles northeast of Jerusalem, he rounded up additional travel companions for muscle and security and left Jerusalem to arrest Christians in Damascus, one of the oldest, continuously inhabited cities in the world.

Since Damascus had been under Roman control for about a hundred years by the time Saul went there, he knew he would be safe and would find Jewish synagogues and communities who would assist him in his quest, especially when they saw his official arrest warrants from the Jewish chief priests. Saul knew if the Christians, who had recently arrived in the city from Israel, had followed the pattern developed in Jerusalem, every synagogue had probably been visited by the followers of Christ who continued to gather in synagogues to pray and to evangelize. If that were the case, locating them would be easy. Saul had a nearly foolproof plan. What could go wrong? His position was strong. He had thought of everything. Nothing could stop him now.

WHO ARE YOU LORD? (9:3-6)

A few days on the well-traveled road to Damascus would have given Saul and his travel companions ample time to decide a strategy for finding and restraining Christians. But just outside the city gates of Damascus, all of his plans unraveled.

Luke describes what happened next, "Now as he went on his way, he approached Damascus, and suddenly a light from heaven shone around him. And falling to the ground he heard a voice saying to him, 'Saul, Saul, why are you persecuting me?'" (9:3-4) Saul saw the sudden flash of light, was knocked to the ground, and experienced temporary *flash-blindness*. The voice from heaven called his name in Aramaic. The voice Saul heard that day changed his plans for the rest of his life. His days of persecuting the Lord's church had come to an abrupt end in a sudden, unexplainable flash of light.

What else could Saul do but answer? "He said, 'Who are you, Lord?' And He said, 'I am Jesus, whom you are persecuting. But rise and enter the city, and you will be told what you are to do'" (vv. 5-6). The appearance of Jesus, alive with power, meant everything Saul had believed had been wrong. His life was about to change.

In that brief conversation with the resurrected Lord, Saul learned something about Jesus and the church he would never forget. Saul had intended to persecute only the followers of Jesus and not Jesus Himself, whom Saul believed was dead. When Jesus confronted Saul, however, He said, "Why are you persecuting Me?" (v. 4). The message of the risen Lord could not be more obvious. Believers have a unique identification with the risen Lord Jesus. Paul would later coin the phrase "in Christ" to describe that spiritual union (Rom. 8:1; 1 Cor. 15:22; 2 Cor. 5:17; Eph. 1:3; Phil. 2:1; Col. 1:2, for example).

On the road to Damascus, Jesus revealed Himself to Saul as the strong, commanding, living Lord. He knocked Saul to the ground, blinded him, chastised him for his role in the persecution, and ordered him to get up, go into the city, and await orders (9:6). The extradition papers Saul was carrying from the chief priests seemed irrelevant, impotent, and pointless now in light of the power of the risen Savior. Saul had just met the King.

THREE DAYS IN THE DARK (9:7-9)

What a difference a few moments can make. Just outside the city gates, Saul had been marching toward the ancient city of Damascus like a hunter on the scent of his prey. He had power, prestige, notoriety, and authority. But by the time he arrived he was blind and unable to guide himself. He had brought other men to help restrain the believers, but the confused travel companions were now needed to hold Saul's hand like a helpless child.

For some people, the loving mercy of Jesus wins the heart of the disciple forever. For the proud, angry, self-reliant kind like Saul, however, Jesus might take a tougher approach in order to establish who is Lord and who is servant. The once defiant Saul, stumbling weakly into the city without sight and needing help to take his next step, was learning a soul-shattering lesson about the power of God.

Once inside Damascus, Saul was led to the home of an otherwise anonymous man named Judas on Straight Street. For the next three days Saul refused food and water as he poured out his heart to God in prayer. We can only imagine the depth of that unrecorded, private prayer summit, when a man came face-to-face with the God he thought he served but had in fact opposed.

While Scripture withholds the transcript of Saul's three-day season of repentance and prayer, we are given a brief glimpse into the message Jesus revealed to Saul while he prayed and fasted. Through a vision, the Lord showed Saul how a disciple of Jesus named Ananias would come and minister to him. God was cultivating the ministry of faith in the future missionary and teaching him about his need for others.

THE HOLY SPIRIT AND A WORLDWIDE MISSION (9:10-22)

Ananias was a believer living in Damascus with a heart sensitive to the leadership of the Lord. In a vision (the Greek word can mean a dream while sleeping, or a detailed revelation seen visually while awake), the Lord told Ananias about Saul praying at the home of Judas. Ananias was to go immediately and lay hands on Saul so he might regain his sight. Ananias had heard about this madman from Jerusalem and was reluctant to go, but Jesus assured him Saul was a chosen instrument, was praying, and would know suffering as part of his new life as His follower.

Once there, Ananias addressed Saul in a way the repentant Pharisee would have never expected. Ananias' first words were a tender term of Christian affection, "Brother Saul" (v. 17). Saul was learning about his new faith and his new people. These people were dependent and humble and yet powerful in the Lord. They were God's true people. The entire experience had to be almost inconceivable for Saul.

Saul regained his sight, was filled with the Holy Spirit, rose from his place of prayer, and was baptized. He never looked back. The old life of hatred and persecution was suddenly and supernaturally a thing of the past. Saul was a changed man.

Saul immediately spent time with the same disciples he had originally come to arrest; he grew in discipleship and enjoyed fellowship with them. Almost immediately he was preaching in the synagogues the message that Jesus is "the Son of God" and "proving that Jesus was the Christ" (vv. 19-22).

Can one man make a difference in the world? Many have, but none have been as single-minded in devotion to Christ as Saul of Tarsus. He intended to destroy Christianity, but instead he became its most visible and most well-known proponent. He went on to write half of the New Testament and personally proclaim the Gospel in Jerusalem, as well as to the vast geographical area of modern Turkey. He then forged ahead to modern Bosnia-Herzegovina in Eastern Europe, and then even farther west to modern Italy. His goal was to preach in Spain, which was the farthest western landmass known to the ancient world and represented the edge of the Roman Empire. Paul was headed to the ends of the earth as he knew it.

Paul the Apostle is the single, greatest example in history of what a follower of Christ can become. He was one changed man who changed the world. Can God bring about that kind of change in a person today? Of course, no one is going to write more Scripture but there are people today who can take the gospel to *the ends of the earth*. God can change anyone who repents of sin and turns to Christ by faith. If the life of Saul of Tarsus teaches us anything, it teaches us no one is beyond the reach of God's grace. God changed Saul to Paul and God can change you too.

Chapter 8
The Vision Expands the Mission
Acts 10:1–11:18

To the dreamer, dreams can be meaningful or bizarre or both. When God wanted the church to reach beyond its self-imposed limitations, He used not one but two dreams or visions to enlarge the faith and expand the perspective of the early church.

Jesus had made it clear from the time of His resurrection that the evangelistic mission of the church would reach "to the end of the earth" (Acts 1:8). However, in spite of His command to take the gospel to the world, several years had passed, and the church was still centralized in Jerusalem and almost exclusively Jewish. The stoning of Stephen probably occurred about five years after the resurrection with the conversion of the Apostle Paul following that event by, at most, a year or two. These two events, combined with an episode in the life of the Apostle Peter which probably occurred about the same time as Paul's conversion, helped widen and clarify the church's understanding of its mission.

When properly understood as interrelated pieces of a larger whole, the three stories (which appear on the surface to be only loosely related) record the church's difficult period of transition and uncertainty about the extent of their mission. In spite of Jesus' clarity about worldwide evangelism, the early church needed dramatic events initiated by outside forces to mobilize them to action. The church had demonstrated no urgency about taking the good news to the Gentiles, so God intervened with actions so intractable, the church was left with no choice but to go to *the ends of the earth* with the gospel.

DOUBLE VISION (10:1-16)

In the story of the church coming to grips with Jesus' worldwide mission there are two men, two visions, and two well-known locations mentioned. The two visions of two strangers were separated by a few days but suddenly collided at the most opportune time.

THE SOLDIER'S VISION (10:1-8)

The first man with a vision was Cornelius, a Roman Centurion, the leader of about one hundred Roman soldiers stationed in the important port city of Caesarea by the Sea (Maritima). The city of Caesarea had an impressive history dating back centuries due to its access to the Mediterranean Sea. About thirty years before the birth of Jesus, Caesar Augustus placed Caesarea under the control of Herod, a young, politically-driven, brilliant but ruthless ruler who was given the title "King of Judea." Herod was an ambitious builder who saw the advantage of improving the coastline of Caesarea Maritima for Roman commercial and military superiority.

The port he built was impressive as "a magnificently engineered project."[12] Today, the archeological excavations of Herod's Caesarea are a tribute to his architectural genius. While the port itself is gone due to destructive earthquakes and changes in leadership over the centuries, the remains of one of the ancient world's great sea ports are still visible after two thousand years.

Along with its impressive harbor, Herod built one of the most beautiful cities in Israel, complete with a magnificent amphitheater (which is still standing), a Roman hippodrome for chariot races, bath houses, a large marketplace, palaces for visiting Roman dignitaries (including himself), and every other amenity available to the wealthy aristocracy of the ancient world. The entire city was cleverly air conditioned, as it was purposely designed to benefit from the cool, east wind which blew perpetually over the gorgeous, lightly foaming waves of the deeply cobalt-blue Mediterranean.

Cornelius lived in Caesarea as an officer of Rome and had become a "God fearer," which was a technical term describing a Gentile who had adopted the Jewish worship and as many of the rituals and customs of Judaism as the work of a Roman soldier might have reasonably permitted. As such, Cornelius is described in Scripture as "a devout man who feared God with all his household, gave alms generously to the people, and prayed continually to God" (10:2). In Jewish life, prayer and giving donations to the poor, called alms, were viewed as the devotional practices of a spiritual man. In His first

---

[12] George W. Knight, "Caesarea," *Holman Illustrated Bible Dictionary* (Nashville: Holman Bible Publishers, 2003), 246-247.

teaching about devotional practices, Jesus Himself, included giving of alms and fasting as three practices He commended and expected His disciples to practice (Matt. 6:1-18).

Cornelius was sincere. He was pursuing God through Judaism and was hungry for more. It was this officer of Rome who received the first of the two visions. Rome had joined with the religious leaders to crucify Jesus, so the reader might expect a harsh judgment against Rome in the Acts' narrative; but as we will repeatedly observe, that is not the case. Luke is surprisingly positive toward Rome. Ultimately, he is writing to an original audience living in the Roman Empire, and the consistent message of Acts is a spiritual narrative supporting world evangelism rather than a political polemic against the empire.

Cornelius' vision was as straightforward as an office memo from the boss. "About the ninth hour of the day he saw clearly in a vision an angel of God come in and say to him, 'Cornelius.' And he stared at him in terror and said, 'What is it, Lord?' And he said to him, 'Your prayers and your alms have ascended as a memorial before God. And now send men to Joppa and bring one Simon who is called Peter. He is lodging with one Simon, a tanner, whose house is by the sea'" (Acts 10:3-6).

The specificity of the vision is similar to the detail given Ananias when he was instructed to visit Saul of Tarsus. There is none of the symbolism present in Peter's vision later in the story. The Roman officer, who regularly gave and received orders, received a direct communication from the Highest Authority. He understood that kind of clarity and direction.

The differences in the way God communicated to the two men in the narrative is a powerful reminder that God knows His people and knows how to speak in different ways to our individual learning styles. The question is: Why did God speak directly to this one man? Were there no other devout God-fearers in Israel? Why did Cornelius receive this direct message from God? Put another way, why did Luke record this particular encounter?

On the one hand, the story of Cornelius may demonstrate if no missionary or witness has reached a person who is otherwise reaching out toward God with all the revelation available to him, God is more than capable of providing more illumination. God, after all, has initiated redemption toward all of us even though most of us are not as keenly aware of God's direct involvement as Cornelius, who received overt instructions in a supernatural vision at 3:00 p.m. one day.

The more obvious reason God worked in a direct inter-vention to bring Cornelius and Peter together highlights the larger story Luke is eager to tell. In just a few days, Cornelius would be the first Gentile convert of the early church. The Gentile soldier, loyal to the Roman Empire and a man whose very livelihood and identity represented the dominance of the Gentile world, serves as a representative of all Gentiles God will save, not only in the book of Acts but for the rest of history.

The vision and response of Cornelius signals a significant shift in the mission of the church and the spread of the gospel. It is not without meaning that it will be Peter, the leader of the early church and the Apostle to the Jews, who will introduce the first Gentile to Christ. Luke's summary of the entire narrative is found later in the story, "And the believers from among the circumcised who had come with Peter were amazed, because the gift of the Holy Spirit was poured out even on the Gentiles" (10:45).

With this event, the direction of Luke's story and, therefore, the remainder of the book of Acts will pivot away from an exclusively Jewish church to a gospel for the entire world. But before that can occur, God has to convince Peter.

THE APOSTLE'S VISION (10:9-20)

The day after the angel appeared to Cornelius, less than forty miles south of Caesarea along the beautiful Mediterranean coast in a small town surrounded today by the modern city of Tel Aviv, the Apostle Peter was having prayer and waiting for lunch. (Peter had originally gone to Joppa in response to an invitation from believers there who were convinced the apostle could raise a dead woman back to life. After God restored the woman's life in response to Peter's prayer, the word spread and an evangelistic opportunity developed throughout the city (See Acts 9:36-38).

Peter stayed several days as a guest in the home of a man in the leather-making industry named Simon the tanner. It was there Peter had the vision that would change the church and change the world.

God revealed the vision to Peter in a more dramatic way than the matter-of-fact directive given to Cornelius. The vision to the apostle is an example of revelation moving from the lesser to the greater. Rather than direct Peter to preach to Gentiles, God began by challenging Peter's lifelong commitment to the Jewish dietary laws. "And he became hungry and wanted something to eat, but while they were preparing it, he fell into a trance and saw the heavens opened and something like a great sheet descending, being let down by its four corners upon the earth. In it were all kinds of animals and reptiles and birds of the air. And there came a voice to him: 'Rise, Peter; kill and eat.' But Peter said, 'By no means, Lord; for I have never eaten anything that is common or unclean.' And the voice came to him again a second time, 'What God has made clean, do not call common.' This happened three times, and the thing was taken up at once to heaven" (10:10-16).

For centuries the Jews had avoided certain types of food forbidden by God in passages such as Leviticus 11:3-23 and Deuteronomy 14:3-21. Why did God instruct Peter to eat foods previously forbidden as a precursor to evangelizing Gentiles? One of the rationales for a dietary regulation for the Jewish people in the first place was to discourage social interaction with pagan nations. If they could not eat the Gentiles' food then the diet served as a natural barrier between Jews and Gentiles. The less contact Jews had with pagan Gentiles and their polytheistic religions, the less risk there was of a Jewish person being influenced by pagan religious practices.

The unique diet of the Jews was a symbol of the Jewish separateness from the rest of the world. "For you are a people holy to the LORD your God, and the LORD has chosen you to be a people for his treasured possession, out of all the peoples who are on the face of the earth. You shall not eat any abomination" (Deut. 14:2-3).

So God presented Peter with a vision of forbidden foods and insisted they were no longer unclean. Peter resisted, but God persisted. God was relaxing the lesser issue of what one eats to prove to Peter the greater issue that he should regard every person as eligible to hear and receive the Gospel of salvation, even if they were not Jewish.

After some thought, Peter understood that message. Upon arriving to Cornelius' home in Caesarea, Peter said, "God has shown me that I should not call any person common or unclean" (Acts 10:28).

THE SERMON

Peter preached to Cornelius and those gathered in his home, reminding them of the death and resurrection of Jesus and the judgment to come. Suddenly the Holy Spirit "fell on all who heard the word" (v. 44). It was like a mini-Pentecost followed by baptisms. The first Gentile had been included into the salvation of Jesus and everything would change.

After Peter's vision, the book of Acts begins turning attention away from Peter to focus more on the missionary ministry of Paul. Through the Apostle Paul, the Gentile world of the Roman Empire will hear the story of Jesus. Luke will take the reader full circle as he spends the next several chapters showing how the church fulfilled Christ's command to go "to the ends of the earth."

Peter's vision, and his explanation of it (Acts 11:1-18), is a reminder to all of us who serve Christ not to become too comfortable in our places of service because God can always change our direction. Sometimes He will make us extremely uncomfortable with new ideas, new challenges, and new dreams until we are willing to obey.

Chapter 9
The Prayer Meeting That Puts the Church on the Map

Acts 13:1-5

The early twentieth century author, S. D. Gordon, once wrote, "You can do *more* than pray, *after* you have prayed. But you *cannot* do more than pray *until* you have prayed."[13] The power of prayer is so prevalent in Acts; there is scarcely an occurrence in the first half of the book where prayer isn't a major contributing factor.

Prayer was the oxygen of the early church. Of the numerous times prayer is mentioned in Acts, it is congregational or group rather than individual prayer being described, with less than a handful of exceptions. Personal prayer in secret, as Jesus taught His disciples in Matthew 6:6, is one of the essential, daily spiritual disciplines of the Christian life. No Christian will walk faithfully with the Lord without developing a personal prayer life. Luke never infers otherwise, but the rapid growth and influence of the early church illustrates how the power of praying with others can change the world.

After the believers were scattered out of Jerusalem, exciting events in Syria paved the way for the major shift in

_____

[13] S.D. Gordon, *Quiet Talks on Prayer,* (Shippensburg, PA: Destiny Image Publishers, Inc., 2003), 12.

the world mission of the church. For one thing, Saul of Tarsus became Paul and emerged as the most important leader in the developing mission to take the Gospel to the "end of the earth" (1:8). At the heart of this important pivot in direction was a world-changing prayer summit.

THE BACKGROUND (ch. 11)

Antioch, Syria is the modern-day city of Antakya in southern Turkey, about five hundred miles northwest of Jerusalem. In the first century it was the third largest city in the Roman Empire, behind only Rome and Alexandria. An estimated population of 500,000 people included a fairly large number of Jews.[14] After the martyrdom of Stephen and the persecution that followed, Jewish Christians in Jerusalem were driven out of the city and went as far north as Antioch.

Once they arrived in the city of Antioch, the believers started to evangelize both the Jews and Gentiles already living there. Those early evangelistic believers were the first followers of Christ to evangelize their own city without apostolic assistance. In fact, when the apostles heard about the number of people turning to Christ in Antioch, they sent the highly regarded disciple Barnabas to investigate the encouraging development (vv. 19-23).

Barnabas was introduced as early as Acts 4:36. His name was Joseph the Levite, a member of the Jewish priesthood

---

[14] I. Howard Marshall, *Acts*, Vol. 5 of The Tyndale New Testament Commentaries (Grand Rapids, MI: Wm. B. Eerdmans Publishing Co., 2000), 200-201.

from the Island of Cyprus. The disciples called him "Barnabas" as a kind of moniker, probably describing the nature of his encouraging messages when he preached or taught other disciples.

He was a generous, faithful, Spirit-filled, and gifted leader who had easily been identified by the apostles, by name, from among the several thousand members of the Jerusalem church. When Barnabas arrived in Antioch, he found a city experiencing spiritual awakening. He preached, taught, and discipled as many as he could, but the opportunity for greater ministry was beyond one leader's capacity.

Barnabas knew a young Bible teacher with remarkable skill and unusual gifts who would be perfect in the nontraditional, spiritually-dynamic environment exploding in the city of Antioch. Saul's preaching had stirred up the city of Damascus. It had been Barnabas who originally recognized Saul's ability and tenacity in spreading the Gospel, so even when the Jerusalem church was afraid of Saul, Barnabas vouched for him.

Barnabas knew the entrepreneurial spirit of the Antioch movement would appeal to Saul's bold style, so he left Antioch in search of Saul to ask for his help. Once inside the Turkish city of Tarsus, Barnabas located the tent-making evangelist and successfully recruited Saul to return with him to one of the most fast-paced and exciting ministry opportunities available since the days of Pentecost.

THE PRAYER SUMMIT (13:1-5)

After more than a year of teaching new believers and evangelizing the thriving metropolitan city of Antioch, Paul, Barnabas, and a gifted group of leaders convened for a prayer summit. Luke introduces them as "prophets and teachers" (v. 1). In the early days of the infant church, prophets and teachers were leaders nearly on par in importance with the apostles (Eph. 4:11). In the case of the Antioch awakening, in the absence of the recognized apostles, the prophets and teachers were the most significant city leaders of the movement.

What would cause this impressive group to retreat from the important spiritual work taking place in Antioch to spend uninterrupted time in prayer? Clearly prayer was the track upon which the train of the early church traveled. They prayed about everything, and in that sense there is nothing unusual about a group spending time in prayer. In fact, the question is not: why did they spend so much time in prayer? The question is: why don't we? Still, beyond the obvious fact that the early church depended heavily upon prayer, is there a more specific reason for this particular prayer meeting?

The clue as to why the group met for prayer might be reasonably deduced from the context. They are identified as important leaders who had spent more than a year building the church at Antioch, and the prayer meeting, as we know it, resulted in a new missionary enterprise. These facts combine to suggest these men had intentionally convened the extended prayer session to seek the Spirit's direction about what they were to do next in the Lord's work.

The other members of the team are relatively unknown to us, but were probably much more well known to Luke's original readers. Assuming the order in which they are listed is a signal of their rank in importance (as is usually the case in the New Testament lists of groups), Saul's name at the end of the list highlights how important and crucial the other four men were to the Antioch mission.

MEET THE TEAM (13:1)

Barnabas is already familiar to the reader. He was officially commissioned by the apostles to provide ministerial leadership to the incredible work of the Spirit in Antioch. His credentials are unquestioned anywhere in Acts. In fact, Luke described him in various passages as a generous encourager and supporter of the church (4:36-37), a man with easy access to the apostles, and he had tremendous, insightful judgement which they trusted without hesitation (9:27). The apostles viewed him as a leader and emissary who could represent the interests of the church as well as those of the apostles (11:22). Luke described him as "a good man, full of the Holy Spirit and of faith" (11:24). Being "full of the Holy Spirit and of faith" is a familiar set of desirable attributes because Luke used the same language to describe the deeply revered martyr, Stephen, (6:5). In addition, no one else in Acts is called "good" except Barnabas. The gifted encourager Barnabas is listed first among the prophets and teachers at the Antioch prayer meeting; therefore, he was the obvious leader.

We know very little about the next three men listed except what can be determined by the terse descriptions Luke provides in the passage itself. Simeon was called *Niger*, which is Latin for black, perhaps indicating he was an African. He may have been none other than the African man, Simon of Cyrene, who helped Jesus carry the cross and was already identified in Luke's gospel (Luke 23:26). Cyrene was in North Africa in modern-day Libya, and Cyrenian believers were part of the original evangelists who flooded into Antioch spreading the good news (Acts 11:20). Lucius of Cyrene, the third leader mentioned, was clearly an African and Manaen, the "lifelong friend of Herod the tetrarch" (13:1) is an apparent example of a disciple from a prestigious, politically well-connected background. Saul is mentioned last.

PRAYER AND THE SPIRIT'S CALL (13:2-4)

The leaders' prayer summit in Antioch is reminiscent of the first disciples praying in the upper room before Pentecost. There appears to be no time limit on the gathering. Only prayer, worship, and fasting filled the agenda. The Holy Spirit directly intervened and the result propelled the church forward in an unprecedented way. The world would forever be changed because of the upper room prayer meeting before Pentecost and the leaders' prayer summit in Antioch.

At the Antioch meeting they were "worshiping" (v. 2), which describes the spiritual discipline of serving the Lord in prayer. The Greek word is the same one used to describe the work done by the priest to facilitate worship in the temple.

Fasting has a long history in Scripture. In addition to the many Old Testament examples of fasting, Jesus said the church would practice fasting after His resurrection (Luke 5:35).

It is clear from the comments later in the passage that the leaders were also praying during the meeting (v. 3). The combination of worship, fasting, and prayer should still characterize the life of those who eagerly desire to see the advancement of God's kingdom.

As they were praying, just as on the day of Pentecost, the Holy Spirit manifested Himself in a powerful way (v. 2). It is a striking scene because the five leaders suddenly heard the voice of the Holy Spirit. *How* He spoke is not explained. We are simply told, "the Holy Spirit said, 'Set apart for me Barnabas and Saul for the work to which I have called them'" (v. 2). There is every reason to assume the Spirit spoke audibly to the entire group. His instructions were direct and still informative for the twenty-first century church. The Spirit claimed *ownership* for the mission of the church and identified Barnabas and Saul as His specially chosen ministers. As a result, the Acts narrative will take a dramatic turn at this point, and the Spirit's work through Paul will dominate the rest of the book.

The Christian outreach to the Gentile world, which has continued for two thousand years, was essentially launched at the prayer summit in Antioch. Most of the church traces its roots to this prayer meeting. It should be remembered, therefore, as an event that changed the world.

THE SPIRIT'S WORK (13:2-4)
Luke had a literary habit of introducing an idea in a subtle way, leaving the idea to address a separate but related subject, then returning to the original concept in a much more dramatic and fully developed storyline. His storytelling prowess was masterful.

In this particular instance, the Spirit identified Barnabas and Saul for the work to which He had called them, but the specific nature of the new mission is temporarily left unexplained to the reader. But based on their response, the mission was clear to the men in the prayer meeting. "Then after fasting and praying they laid their hands on them and sent them off" (v. 3).

LESSONS OF ANTIOCH (13:1-4)
The consistent pattern developed in the groundbreaking action of the early church is clear. The church prayed persistently about opportunities, as well as obstacles with equal passion. The people depended upon the direct and conspicuous leadership of the Holy Spirit working through gifted leaders and average believers. They focused on plain-spoken teaching of Scripture to explain the cross of Christ and His miraculous resurrection, and they gathered in groups for mutual support wherever they went.

In light of our complex lives, it may seem as if praying and expecting the Holy Spirit to work gets lost today. Yet the pattern of prayer and waiting on God has never been improved upon. The early believers put the church on the map of the Roman Empire in one generation with none of our modern advantages. They had limited technical and financial resources, but their passion for prayer and the work of the Spirit remain as an inviting model for contemporary believers who want to change the world.

Chapter 10
Jesus in Europe
Acts 16:6-46

In the beautiful cities of Europe today, from the legendary architecture of Athens to the warm Puerta del Sol of Madrid, whether strolling the Ha'penny Bridge over the River Liffey in Dublin or barreling full speed down the Autobahn in Germany, you are sure to see churches. In fact, all twenty-eight nations of the current European Union are officially Christian. It wasn't always that way. The Christian history of Europe began two thousand years ago when the Holy Spirit interrupted the plans of Paul, an ambitious missionary with his sights set on other shores.

At the leaders' prayer summit at Antioch, the Holy Spirit had spoken forcefully about the ministry of Barnabas and Saul, "to which I have called them" (13:2). If there can be any lingering doubt about the deity of the Holy Spirit, His person-hood, or His direct involvement with the church and its mission, surely His clear ownership of the Gentile mission ends the debate. The Spirit claimed personal responsibility in the choice of the two missionaries and the work He called them to do. Over the next few years the two zealous friends would repeatedly learn that the Spirit freely changes our plans when it suits God's purposes, even if He has to wake us in the middle of the night with a vision to arrest our attention.

OUR PLANS/HIS PLANS (16:1-9)

Paul and Barnabas began their work immediately after the prayer summit (ch. 13) and continued traveling along a mostly predictable geographical route. The travelers made their way on a circular sweep through the prominent cities of the region of Galatia, in what is today central Turkey. They evangelized as they traveled between well-known cities, which were all in a relatively close proximity to each other, before returning to Antioch. The areas they traveled were never far from the ministry home base of Antioch or Cyprus, where Barnabas was from, or Tarsus, Paul's hometown. The route made perfect sense.

After a trip to Jerusalem to attend an important meeting convened by the apostles and elders to discuss Gentile evangelism, Paul and Barnabas returned again to Antioch, the central hub of mission operations. By this time about three years had transpired since Paul and Barnabas had started traveling, having spent about two years in central Turkey on the first mission trip. Naturally Paul had begun thinking strategically about their next venture. After all, about a year had passed since they had returned from that first mission trip through Galatia in modern Turkey, and Paul was growing concerned about the spiritual health of the churches they had planted.

Paul and Barnabas famously disagreed about who should have the right to travel with them on the next trip, so Barnabas took John Mark (the eventual author of the shortest Gospel) and left for the familiar territory of home on the Isle of Cyprus. Paul enlisted Silas and headed north over the mountains in the direction of Tarsus, his own hometown (15:36-41).

As he traveled into Galatia, Paul met Timothy, the exemplary young disciple who was ready to go with Paul and the mission team. So they traveled farther west toward what was then called *Asia*, in modern-day western Turkey. They were blazing new trails and hoping to evangelize new areas, but the Holy Spirit restricted them from preaching in the areas any farther ahead of them (16:6). So they headed to ancient Bithynia, in the northernmost part of Turkey. The region is a vacation destination today, with white sand beaches, and it is known for the verdant coasts falling into the aqua waters of the curiously named Black Sea. Once again, without explanation, "the Spirit of Jesus did not allow them" (v. 7).

Paul had a clear sense of where he was going, but as is frequently the case, the Spirit will block most obvious and sensible plans and the most reasonable agendas, even plans conceived by those who want nothing more than to do His will. Every Christian eventually learns a lesson about the Spirit's leadership as taught in the revelation to the prophet Isaiah,

> *For my thoughts are not your thoughts,*
> *neither are your ways my ways, declares the Lord.*
> *For as the heavens are higher than the earth,*
> *so are my ways higher than your ways*
> *and my thoughts than your thoughts. (Isa. 55:8-9).*

In other words, if we plan to follow the Spirit's plans we have to plan on surrendering our plans! The Spirit's reason for changing Paul's direction would become more obvious as the team continued on.

Following the most logical route forward, Paul forged on several miles to the northwestern coastal city of Troas. Exhausted from travel Paul found a place to rest for the night, but his sleep was prematurely interrupted by a vision that would lead to something new. The readers of Acts have become familiar, by this point, with sudden changes in the direction of the narrative. In Paul's vision he simply saw "a man of Macedonia," but he had a message with an irresistible attraction for Paul: "Come over to Macedonia and help us" (v. 9). Luke doesn't attempt to explain or identify who the "man of Macedonia" was, but in a sense the mysterious "man of Macedonia" represents hundreds of millions of Christians of European descent who can trace their spiritual heritage back, in part, to the vision of that anonymous Macedonian man.

Paul had traveled hundreds of arduous miles through mountainous, sparsely-populated regions with little to show for it. He had finally arrived at the edge of the world he knew. It was there, when he had exhausted every logical option, the Spirit issued a clear direction forward. The Spirit led Paul's team through frustration and *closed doors*, but in His timing, in an unexpected way, the future and God's plan seemed obvious.

Paul had not originally planned to go to Troas. His willingness to keep going, however, in spite of initial setbacks, brought him to the exact place he needed to be in order to hear the Spirit's call and take the next step in the missionary enterprise. God obviously wanted the team to go to Macedonia in Greece. The previous times, when the Spirit had said no to other directions, made more sense in light of the new directive to journey into Greece. The gospel had never been to Europe. The next steps taken by Paul's team, in response to the Spirit's leadership, would change the world. Paul was taking Jesus to Europe. Or should we say, Jesus was taking Paul?

JESUS IN EUROPE (16:10-15)

Paul's team wasted no time leaving Troas, and within a few days they were in Philippi, "a leading city of the district of Macedonia" (v. 12). Along the way, the team had picked up a new member. For the first time in the book of Acts, Luke almost unnoticeably included himself in the story as he changed the narrative to the first person saying, "immediately we sought to go into Macedonia" (v.10). Once in Philippi Luke wrote, "We remained in this city some days" (v.12). Paul had assembled an impressive team, including Silas, Timothy, and Luke. The four of them took the story of Jesus to Europe.

On the Jewish Sabbath, the team took a short walk outside the city limits to the Gangites River where they expected to find a small group of Jewish men. Evidently there was no synagogue in Philippi, which would have required at least ten Jewish men to form.[15] In the absence of a synagogue,

---

[15] John B. Polhill, *Acts*, The New American Commentary, vol. 26 (Nashville: Broadman Press, 1992), 348.

Paul and the team went to the river expecting to find a place of prayer. The running water of the river, which today is little more than a gentle, shallow stream, would have provided one of the requirements Jewish worshippers needed for ceremonial washing. Before the Sabbath Day ended, the River became the place of Christian baptism.

As usual in Acts, even though it is subtle, prayer plays a role in the larger story arch in nearly every evangelistic event: Before Pentecost the people prayed (1:14). Before the healing at the Beautiful Gate, and the evangelism that followed, the apostles were headed to prayer (3:1-26). When the church stalled in growth the apostles recommitted themselves to prayer, and the church started growing again (6:4-7). Saul of Tarsus spent three days in prayer followed by effective evangelistic witness (9:11-22). Peter was praying when the vision came to evangelize Gentiles, followed by the salvation of a Roman Centurion's family (10:9-44). When the vision for missions came to the leaders in Antioch, they were praying, and what followed was the highly successful first missionary journey of Paul and Barnabas (chs. 13–14). In Acts, even when it seems indirect, Luke makes it impossible for us to separate evangelism from prayer.

In Philippi, Paul's team went to "a place of prayer" and found a small prayer group, consisting of a few women. What happened next, at the place of prayer on the river bank, changed the world. (16:3)

THE FIRST CONVERTS IN EUROPE (16:11-15)

Lydia was a powerful international merchant whose clients included kings and priests. Today, we would probably regard her as the CEO of a Fortune 500 company specializing in high-end fashion for a select, wealthy, short list of customers. She had shattered the *glass ceiling* at a time when it was considerably more difficult to do than it is today. She was in charge of the acquisition and distribution of a unique and highly sought after product controlled by a multinational organization, headquartered near the Aegean Sea.

Luke identified Lydia as a "seller of purple goods" (v. 14). Only royalty or pagan priests could afford the purple products made from the murex shell, harvested from the Aegean Sea or tediously extracted in small amounts from the dark juice of the madder root, found in a few places in Africa, the Mid-East, and Europe. Thyatira was well known for its guild of purple manufacturers, approximately 250 miles from Philippi.[16]

In addition to being a wealthy Gentile business woman Lydia was, like Cornelius in Caesarea, a "worshiper of God" (v. 14). All the mission team members (including Luke) spoke individually to the women at the prayer meeting (v. 13) and probably joined them in prayer, but at some point, Paul took the lead in explaining the good news of Jesus. Lydia was acutely interested, and "the Lord opened her heart" (v. 14) to receive the forgiveness and salvation. Paul had arrived in

---

[16] Ibid., 349.

Europe less than a week earlier, and God had led him to an open heart. The Western world would never be the same.

The baptism that followed her salvation is typical of Acts. Every person baptized in the book of Acts was baptized at the time of their conversion. The river was ideal for the practice. Today the location of the baptism is fairly easy to determine. Although the gates of Philippi are no longer standing, some of the later ruins have been carefully reconstructed. Standing among the ruins, looking toward the trees growing on the river bank, it is easy to imagine what happened that day. About a mile from the city limits, in a shallow place in the river surrounded now by tall, leafy shade trees, the first convert on European soil met Christ and was baptized.

THE WORLD BEYOND PHILLIPI

Paul may not have recognized the significance of the Gospel going to Europe, since Macedonia was as much a part of the Roman Empire as Antioch, Tarsus, or Jerusalem.[17] Luke, however, does seem to recognize a new barrier had once again been crossed. Two thousand years later, we can see the influence of Jesus on the Western world's history. When Paul and the first mission team followed the leadership of the Spirit into Europe, they started a movement that changed the world, even if they didn't know it at the time.

The Holy Spirit led the mission team to do the unexpected, in order to reach unreached people. He hasn't changed

---

[17] John R. W. Stott, *The Message of Acts, T*he Bible Speaks Today (Downers Grove, IL.: InterVarsity Press, 1990), 258.

in two thousand years. He still says no to some of our plans, even though our motives are pure and our logic is sound. If we expect to follow the Spirit's leadership, we can expect Him to prevent our plans from succeeding, if those plans contradict God's superior plans for us. Learning to accept no as an answer from God is essential to Christian growth and part of following the Spirit's lead.

Obeying the leadership of the Spirit may not always seem sensible at the moment, but following even when they didn't understand how significant their steps would be led Paul's team to change the world. We can only guess when the next disciple, following the Lord in a direction she cannot under-stand, will change the world again.

Chapter 11
The Mission to Mars Hill
Acts 17:16–19:1-41

Strange things can happen in unexpected places. In a small southern town, a silent epidemic of drug use was creeping into the community.

Most of the older residents were still unaware it was happening. But drugs were there, and young people knew it. The kids in the youth group confided in their youth minister, who had been a drug abuser himself before he was a Christian. Other young people had witnessed to him back then, and his life had been changed. He was convinced the same thing could happen now if he could evangelize the local drug pushers. So he learned all he could; he prayed about it, and he decided on a plan.

The drug distribution was not a sophisticated operation. Near the town square, late at night when the shops had long been closed and the lights were out downtown, cars drove slowly through the dark streets. The drivers watched for young men who were standing alone on the dark corners of the town's empty sidewalks, ready to sell drugs. It happened that way every night.

The youth minister recruited his Christian friends who were willing to evangelize the men on the corners. We met at the minister's apartment and prayed for a few hours. Around midnight we headed into the streets to share Christ with low-level drug dealers standing in the shadows near the town square.

Once there, we split up to reach whomever we could. I spotted a man in his early twenties who was standing almost motionless on the corner by a darkened shop, away from any light. He was smoking a cigarette and staring across the street. What could he possibly be doing there? I decided to find out.

Maybe he thought I wanted to buy drugs. He appeared pensive and rigid as I approached him. He barely looked in my direction. It was chilly that night, and he had one hand inside his jacket pocket as he stoically smoked a cigarette with the other. His long hair was combed back and reached nearly to his shoulders. Standing alone in the shadows on an empty street made no sense. He was there for only one reason.

I was nervous but determined, so I started talking. I was there to evangelize, and he immediately was certain I was not there to buy drugs. I was quoting Scripture and telling him about sin and the cross. He looked angry, but he stood perfectly still, except for the repetitious motion of smoking a cigarette. He wouldn't even look at me. It was as if I wasn't there.

In a matter of minutes a police car pulled up, and an officer dressed in dark blue got out of his car and shined a flashlight on me. He walked directly to me and demanded to know what I was doing. He asked for my identification, and I showed him my driver's license and gospel tracts. I told the police officer I was having a conversation about Christ with the man standing next to me. My long-haired, quiet friend never moved, and he never said a word. He just kept smoking. The policeman said nothing to the man with the cigarette. He only informed me I was disturbing the peace, and unless I wanted to spend the night in jail, I needed to leave right then.

Disturbing the peace? Whose peace was I disturbing? It was after midnight on a street corner in a nonresidential part of downtown. I wasn't loud; I was only talking to one man. But I had a choice that night—I could start a jail ministry or I could move along. I chose the latter.

Sometimes, we can do the right thing for the right reason, and it all seems to go wrong. Even the Apostle Paul experienced the sting of rejection.

EVANGELISM IN ATHENS (17:16-34)

As a young Pharisee, Paul had earned his reputation as the persecutor of the church. Now, however, he frequently found himself on the other side of the persecution. He had been threatened with death in Damascus, beaten and jailed in Philippi, escorted out of Thessalonica at night to avoid a mob, and forced out of Berea for the same reason. But what he encountered in Athens was completely different. He was ridiculed.

Athens, Greece has a history that rivals any ancient city in the world, but by the time Paul arrived its glory days were fading. Greek was still the most common language of the Empire, but the Romans were in power now and Greek dominance in the world was, in most ways, a thing of the past.[18]

Athens, however, was still the center of art, architecture, and philosophy. For days Paul had walked alone through the streets of Athens observing their religious statues and idols. The prevalence of the idolatry throughout the city "provoked" him (v. 16). The word *provoked* comes from a Greek root word meaning "sharp" and suggests Paul felt an emotion akin to a stabbing pain. He was irritated and angry, so he responded.

Paul started his evangelistic ministry in the Jewish synagogues wherever he traveled. It made sense. He knew and understood the audience. He also cared deeply about them (Rom. 9:1-5). On the Sabbath he found a Jewish synagogue and started preaching.

In addition, he practiced a strategy of open-air debate in the "marketplace" (v. 17). Inside the synagogue he was no threat to the city, but in the marketplace sharing Christ, his message was threatening and unheard of in a city that prided itself on knowing the latest trends in philosophy (v. 21).

In the marketplace, where people gathered to debate, two groups with deep roots in the city's storied history of philosophy were represented. Epicureans believed gods were unconcerned with humanity. Therefore, their philosophy

---

[18] I. Howard Marshall, *Acts*, The Tyndale New Testament Commentaries (Grand Rapids, MI: William B. Eerdmans Publishing Company), 283.

was built upon a materialistic view of life. They did not believe in a *spiritual life*. Instead, they focused on avoiding pain and passion in this life. The Stoics were pantheists who lived for reason and self-sufficiency.[19] To the philosophers Paul's message seemed like "babble," a word describing scavenger birds who live by picking up seeds wherever they find them. As applied to Paul's preaching, it meant there was no thought or reason behind the message—as if Paul's thoughts were merely stray ideas collected from a variety of unrelated sources and spewed out, making no sense at all. They thought Paul was ignorant and lacked any legitimate credentials. They were not impressed.

Others present in the crowd, however, suspected he was preaching a new religion since he talked about Jesus and the resurrection. In light of the conversation generated around Paul, he was invited to speak to the leading philosophers of the city at a place called the *Areopagus*, which is also translated as "Mars Hill." It was named after the Greek god Ares and the Roman counterpart Mars, the gods of war. It was a fitting place name since Paul was invited to speak his mind, and he would introduce the Christian message into the battle of ideologies.

It is at that precise point where the events in Paul's day intersect with the need of our time. We live in a culture of radically different philosophies. For example, in the United States people are polarized about politics. Liberals and conservatives differ on almost every issue of the day, and the

---

[19] John B. Polhill, *Acts*, The New American Commentary, vol. 26 (Nashville: Broadman Press, 1992), 366.

differences are pronounced, vocal, and even hostile. Why? Some may not consciously consider it, but we are all influenced by worldviews and philosophies. In this mix of battling extremes, Christians are called to evangelize. We must enter and engage the marketplace of ideas, and we must boldly proclaim our message.

Preaching in our churches is foundational to our commitment to discipleship, but it may be less effective as an evangelistic strategy as the culture grows more secular and less likely to ever attend church services. Christians, therefore, must be equipped to evangelize outside the church whenever we interact with others.

PAUL'S MESSAGE ON MARS HILL (17:22-34)

The steps engraved into the stone hillside leading up to the top of the Areopagus (Mars Hill) are rounded and slick today, after hundreds of thousands, or perhaps millions, of people have climbed them through the years. It is almost impossible to ascend them now, and coming down can feel more like a slide than a set of steps.

The top of Mars Hill is uneven and difficult to walk across as well, but the view is breathtaking. High above, yet not at all far from Mars Hill is the Parthenon, which was more than four hundred years old by the time Paul went to Athens. In addition, part of the sprawling modern city of Athens is visible from the view atop the solid stone hill. But architecture and city views were irrelevant to Paul. He wasn't in Athens for a sightseeing vacation; he was on a mission.

Paul's message to the philosophers started with an observation about the many idols in the city. He reminded them they had a shrine to an "unknown god," and Paul had come to make God known. His evangelistic *outline* started with creation and man's moral responsibility to God as the Creator. Paul even quoted from a poem by the second century BC poet, Aratus, who lived in Athens at the time of the Stoic philosophy's development, but who had been born in Paul's native Cilicia[20] He also quoted from an ancient poem written by Epimenides, who had a connection to Athens seven hundred years earlier. Obviously, Paul was trying to establish a relationship with his erudite audience.

He moved quickly to the issues of repentance and God's judgment, immediately followed by a declaration of the resurrection. At that point, some of those present reacted with mockery and Paul's time was up.

Like the voices in our culture that ridicule the idea of the supernatural as mere superstition left over from a prescientific past, the Athenians refused to listen. Paul had made an impact on a few, and they followed him out from the group and became believers.

Though he was mocked, Paul continued the mission, undeterred by the negative response. We must do the same.

---

[20] F.F. Bruce, *The Book of Acts* (Revised), The New International Commentary on the New Testament (Grand Rapids, MI: William B. Eerdmans Publishing Company, 1988), 339.

EVANGELISM TODAY

Paul's message before the philosophers may be instructive for our evangelistic presentations today. He tried to build a relational bridge but wasted no time getting to the main point. It's true that his message was not as successful that day as it had been in other places, but none of us can name a single person who ridiculed him. Those people are long forgotten, but every week hundreds of people from around the world visit Mars Hill because Paul had been there. Our message will not always be received but one day it will be vindicated.

In a culture that refuses to listen, we must not stop talking. We cannot surrender our mission, even when we are persecuted, misunderstood, or mocked. Our resolve to reach the world must not change, in spite of how we are received.

As witnesses, we may not always see the Gospel's progressing in the world as we would hope to see it. Even Paul experienced rejection and ridicule, but he recognized God was still at work. We may also experience occasional setbacks. We may be ridiculed or persecuted for believing and proclaiming the Gospel. We may do the right thing for the right reason and get what appears to be the wrong result. God, however, is responsible for the final victory, and we are called to remain faithful. At this very moment, in ways we may not understand, God is working through His church, and His church is still changing the world.

Chapter 12
The Chains That
Changed the World
Acts 21–28

Robert F. Kennedy was running for president and had
planned a stop in Indianapolis to speak to a large,
predominantly African-American audience. That night, April
4, 1968, would be unlike any other campaign stop. Kennedy,
standing on the back of a flatbed truck, had the grim task of
telling the audience that civil rights leader Dr. Martin Luther
King Jr. had been assassinated in Memphis that same night.
The crowd gasped audibly when he shared the terrible news.

The large crowd listened quietly as Senator Kennedy
calmly described his admiration for Dr. King. He reminded
them he lost a brother to an assassin's rifle. He spoke from his
heart without notes and shared their grief.

There was racial violence in other cities that night but
not in Indianapolis. During Kennedy's unplanned speech a
moment stands out which clearly drew from his own, recent,
personal suffering. Robert Kennedy said, "My favorite poet
was Aeschylus, and he once wrote:

Even in our sleep, pain which cannot forget
falls drop by drop upon the heart,

until, in our own despair,
against our will,
comes wisdom
through the awful grace of God."[21]

Senator Kennedy reminded the audience suffering can actually serve God's greater purpose in our lives. Suffering, after all, rather than success, connects us all.

The Christian faith has been shaped by suffering. From the agonizing death of Christ on the cross, to the martyrdom of the apostles, to the brutality against defenseless Christians today, our story has been written with blood.

THE CHAINS OF THE APOSTLE

The Roman Empire was evangelized from a prison cell. Suffering for the sake of the gospel, however, did not come as a surprise. For example, only a few days after Jesus appeared to Paul for the first time, the Lord told Ananias, "I will show him how much he must suffer for the sake of my name" (Acts 9:16).

That promise was fulfilled. Paul became an incredibly effective spokesman for Christ, able to evangelize Jewish leaders, wealthy Gentiles as well as slaves, Greek philosophers, Roman soldiers, and more. He was a disciple-maker who recruited and trained the next generation of pastors

---

[21] National Public Radio. "Robert Kennedy: Delivering News of King's Death," accessed February 22, 2016, http://www.npr.org/2008/04/04/89365887/robert-kennedy-delivering-news-of-kings-death .

and missionaries, such as Timothy, Titus, and Silas. He even discipled a Gentile physician and historian, who would later write more than 25 percent of the New Testament, including the book of Acts.

Paul practiced cross-cultural evangelism and church planting, and he devoted himself to a life of nearly endless travel. He wrote thirteen books of the New Testament, which have influenced the theology and practices of the church for two thousand years.

He did all of that, and more, while being threatened repeatedly with mob violence. He was frequently escorted, secretly, out of towns for his own protection. He was stoned and left for dead, often beaten, hated, and ridiculed—and that lifestyle of perpetual suffering reflects his ministry before he spent years in prison! Paul evangelized the empire, in spite of constant physical and psychological abuse.

Is a willingness to suffer for Christ a discipline churches in our culture have forgotten? Can we hope to see renewal in the church and spiritual awakening if our own comfort takes precedence over all else?

How many of us are ready to say, with Paul, "Indeed, I count everything as loss because of the surpassing worth of knowing Christ Jesus my Lord. For his sake I have suffered the loss of all things and count them as rubbish, in order that I may gain Christ" (Phil. 3:8). Are we prepared to choose his life goals as our own "that I may know him and the power of his resurrection, and may share his sufferings, becoming like him in his death"? (Phil. 3:10).

Paul, like few other figures in history, turned suffering, torture, and imprisonment into a platform to advance the gospel. The book of Acts, which details so many victories and miracles, concludes with the church's principal spokesman in prison, yet fully engaged in ministry to the world. Paul's example of suffering, while simultaneously flourishing in ministry, is a model for evangelism and missions today's Christians may be called to embrace.

CHAINS IN JERUSALEM (21:30–23:22)

The Holy Spirit made it clear to Paul he would face imprisonment and sufferings in Jerusalem (20:22-24). For years he had evangelized Gentiles throughout the Roman Empire and, as a result, the Jewish leaders hated him and wanted him dead.

When Paul went to the temple for the last time, the Jewish leaders dragged him out and tried to beat him to death on the spot. The ensuing riot drew the attention of the Roman authorities who saved Paul in order to keep the peace.

The Romans arrested him and put him in chains, but Paul convinced them to let him speak to the Jewish crowd. Speaking to the Jews in their native language, he reminded them of his Jewish pedigree. He explained how he had heard the voice of Jesus on the way to persecute Christians in Damascus. When he told them Jesus was sending him to evangelize Gentiles, the crowd demanded his death.

The Romans took him away and prepared to flog him, but Paul announced he was a Roman citizen. Flogging a Roman, especially without a trial, would be illegal.

The next day the Romans delivered Paul to the Jewish rulers, where he created another stir by shouting he was on trial for believing God would raise the dead. Since Jewish opinion was divided about the existence of an afterlife, the rulers got into a rowdy internal debate and the Roman authorities, once again, rescued Paul. The next night, the Lord appeared to Paul and assured him, "Take courage, for as you have testified to the facts about me in Jerusalem, so you must testify also in Rome." (23:11)

CHAINS BEFORE FELIX (23:23–24:27)
Since the Jews had hatched a plot to assassinate Paul, the Romans escorted Paul to Caesarea By the Sea to imprison him and calm the tumult in the city of Jerusalem. Once there, Paul offered a defense before Felix, the governor of Judea.

Felix was fairly familiar with aspects of the Christian movement, so he knew about Jesus. His curiosity about what was happening in the population he governed might explain why he wanted a private audience with Paul after the initial trial.

One of Felix's wives was Jewish, a daughter of one of the Herod's, and together, in private, they asked Paul to explain more about Christ. Did Paul plead for his freedom once he had a secluded meeting with Felix? No. He preached the Gospel directly, and when he pressed the issues of righteousness and the coming judgment, Felix was unnerved. We get our word *phobia* from the word Luke used to describe the reaction of the governor to Paul's message. Felix was terrified when he considered falling under the judgment of God. Paul was the prisoner, but it was the conscience of Felix on trial as Paul freely spoke.

Paul's willingness to preach the gospel without fear should inspire us to speak for Christ, in every situation, with courage. The gospel is more powerful than politics or prisons!

CHAINS BEFORE FESTUS (25:1-12)

Felix met with Paul privately for about two years, but his motives were not always pure. In addition to wanting to hear about Christ, Felix was hoping for a bribe from Paul in exchange for his release. In the absence of a payoff, and to keep the Jews happy, Felix left Paul in prison for the next governor, who was appointed as his replacement.

Festus, the new governor in Caesarea, was unconcerned about Jewish theological debates. For Festus, the entire issue between the Jewish leaders and Paul was merely, "certain points of dispute with him about their own religion and about a certain Jesus, who was dead, but whom Paul asserted to be alive" (25:19).

Neither Felix nor Festus, the Roman officials, believed Paul was guilty of a crime against Rome but held him to keep the peace with the nation they governed. To avoid being sent back to Jewish custody, however, Paul exercised his rights and appealed his case to Caesar.

Festus later said he would have released Paul if he had not appealed to Caesar, which apparently was an irrevocable appeal. Had Paul made an error in appealing to Caesar? Not at all. He knew a trial before Caesar was an opportunity to preach the gospel to the most powerful audience in the world. Jesus had already promised Paul that an audience with Caesar would be accomplished by the plan of God (23:11).

If Felix had been interested in Christ, Festus had been indifferent. Still, Paul made sure they both heard about the resurrection of Christ. As witnesses, we may not always have a receptive audience, but our job is to present the message.

CHAINS BEFORE AGRIPPA (25:13–26:32)
Agrippa was the "king of the Jews." His family had a long and murderous history with Christianity. His father, Herod Agrippa I, executed the Apostle James and imprisoned Peter in hopes of achieving the same outcome (12:1-4). Agrippa's grandfather was Herod the Great, the paranoid, bloodthirsty king in the story of the magi (Matt. 2:1-16).

When Agrippa came to Caesarea for an official visit, his sister Bernice accompanied him. It was an open secret; the relationship between Agrippa and Bernice was an incestuous scandal.[22]

When Paul appeared before Agrippa and Bernice, Festus and the leaders of the city were present. Paul was in chains and had been in prison for more than two years, but without a hint of intimidation he preached one of his most engaging, evangelistic messages. Rather than attacking the obvious moral failures of Agrippa, Paul spoke positively about Agrippa's knowledge of Jewish customs and practices.

Paul explained how he met Jesus on the road to Damascus and that Jesus had commissioned Paul to take the Gospel to both Jews and Gentiles. He presented the gospel of Christ's suffering and resurrection; at which point, Festus couldn't control himself and blurted out, "Paul, you are out of your mind; your great learning is driving you out of your mind" (Acts 26:24). Paul brushed aside the governor's accusation and continued his appeal to the king. Deftly, Paul turned the conversation directly to Agrippa's spiritual condition. The prisoner on trial put the "king of the Jews" on the spot by asking him, publicly, if he believed the Hebrew prophets!

What happened next demonstrates the power of Paul's message. Agrippa, the king, was on the defensive. "And Agrippa said to Paul, 'In a short time would you persuade me to be a Christian?' And Paul said, 'Whether short or long, I would to God that not only you but also all who hear me this day might become such as I am—except for these chains'"

---

[22] John B. Polhill, *Acts*, The New American Commentary, vol. 26 (Nashville, TN., Broadman Press, 1992), 493.

(vv. 28-29). Imagine that moment. Paul, though on trial, seemed to control the proceedings as he fearlessly delivered his message. Even in chains he considered life in Christ superior to any life without Christ, even the privileged life of a king.

Paul's selfless insistence on proclaiming Christ, in every situation, challenges our priorities. Our message cannot consist of complaining about the conditions of the world or the world's treatment of us. Our message is not about us at all.

CHAINED BUT UNHINDERED (chs. 27–28)

The book of Acts ends with Paul as a prisoner in Rome awaiting a trial before Caesar, yet enjoying a certain amount of freedom, with only a soldier to guard him. He even rented a house, or a room, capable of hosting large crowds (28:23). He stayed in Rome at least two years under house arrest, daily preaching "the Lord Jesus Christ" (v. 31).

In the beginning of Acts, Jesus promised the gospel would go "to the end of the earth" (1:8). From Luke's vantage point, Paul's constant preaching and disciple-making in the Empire's capital city was the clearest indication the promise of Jesus was being fulfilled.

The last word in the book of Acts sums up the confidence the early church had in Jesus and His message. No matter what chains the world had used to shackle the church, the proclamation of the gospel was still "with all boldness and without hindrance" (28:31).

With that, Luke's summary was complete. No power on earth could stop the Gospel or the people of God. What was true then is true now. The church changes the world.